THE XXL AIR FRYER RECIPE BOOK UK

Quick & Delicious Air Fryer Recipes for Everyday
Enjoyment I incl. Vegan & Vegetarian I Nutritional
Facts I Family Favourites Collection

EDWARD MARTIN

TABLE OF CONTENTS

EXCLUSIVE BONUS

40 Weight Loss Recipes

&

14 Days Meal Plan

Scan the QR-Code and receive
the FREE download:

INTRODUCTION

1. Understanding the Air Fryer Revolution

The air fryer has revolutionized the way we cook, offering a healthier alternative to traditional frying methods without sacrificing taste or texture. At its heart, the air fryer uses rapid air circulation to cook food, creating a crispy, golden exterior much like deep frying but with significantly less oil. This technology has made it possible to enjoy your favourite fried foods with up to 80% less fat. This ingenious appliance works by circulating hot air around the food at high speeds, ensuring even cooking and a satisfying crunch. The result is not only a reduction in fat but also quicker cooking times and fewer messes compared to traditional frying.

The versatility of the air fryer is remarkable. Whether you're cooking vegetables, meats, or even baking, the air fryer can handle a wide array of recipes with ease. It allows for a more health-conscious approach to preparing meals, making it a valuable addition to any kitchen. The air fryer's popularity can be attributed to its ability to deliver crispy, flavourful results with minimal effort. It has quickly become a favourite for those seeking convenience and healthier options in their cooking routine.

2. Healthy Eating Made Easy with Air Frying

One of the greatest benefits of using an air fryer is its ability to support a healthier lifestyle without compromising on flavour. Traditional frying methods often require large amounts of oil, leading to meals that are higher in fat and calories. Air frying, on the other hand, uses just a fraction of the oil, or in many cases, none at all, making it a great tool for those who want to reduce their fat intake while still enjoying crispy, delicious food. With the air fryer, you can prepare a wide variety of dishes that are not only lower in fat but also packed with nutrients. Roasting vegetables, grilling lean meats, and even baking are all made easier and healthier with this versatile appliance. By retaining more nutrients through quicker cooking times and reduced oil, air-fried meals can play a big role in a balanced diet.

For those with dietary restrictions or specific health goals, air frying offers flexibility. Whether you're aiming to cut down on saturated fats, lower your calorie intake, or increase your vegetable consumption, the air fryer makes it simple to adapt your favourite meals to meet your needs.

Ultimately, air frying combines the best of both worlds – the ability to enjoy indulgent, crispy textures with far fewer calories, all while encouraging healthier eating habits in everyday life.

3. Mastering Air Fryer Controls and Functions

Getting acquainted with your air fryer's controls and functions is the key to unlocking its full potential. Here's a detailed guide to help you navigate these features effectively.

Temperature Control:
The temperature dial or digital setting allows you to select the ideal heat level for different types of food. Most recipes will require a temperature between 160°C and 200°C. For crispy results, preheat the air fryer to the desired temperature before adding your ingredients.

Timer Function:
The timer lets you set the cooking duration, usually ranging from 1 minute to 60 minutes, depending on the model. It's essential to set the timer accurately to prevent overcooking or undercooking your food. Many air fryers will beep when the cooking time is up, alerting you to check your food.

Pre-set Programs:
Many air fryers come with pre-set programs for specific types of dishes such as chips, chicken, or vegetables. These pre-sets are programmed with optimal cooking times and temperatures for each type of food. While they provide a convenient starting point, you might still need to adjust settings based on your personal preferences and the quantity of food.

Fan Speed and Convection Mode:
Some advanced models offer adjustable fan speeds or a convection mode. The fan circulates hot air around the food, ensuring even cooking and a crispy finish. Using the convection mode can be particularly useful for baking or roasting.

Dehydrate and Bake Functions:
If your air fryer includes a dehydrate function, it allows you to make dried fruits, jerky, or other dehydrated snacks. The bake function turns your air fryer into a mini oven, perfect for making cakes, muffins, or pastries.

Basket and Rack Placement:
Understanding how to position the basket or racks is crucial for even cooking. For optimal

airflow, avoid overcrowding the basket and place food in a single layer if possible. If your air fryer has multiple racks, be sure to rotate them halfway through cooking for consistent results.

Cleaning and Maintenance:

Regularly clean your air fryer to maintain its performance. Most removable parts are dishwasher safe, but always refer to the manufacturer's instructions. Wipe down the interior and exterior with a damp cloth to remove any residual oil or food particles.

With these controls and functions, you'll enhance your cooking efficiency and achieve consistently great results with your air fryer.

4. Essential Safety Tips for Air Fryer Cooking

Using an air fryer is straightforward, but like any kitchen appliance, it's important to follow safety guidelines to ensure a safe and enjoyable cooking experience. Here are some key safety tips to keep in mind:

Read the Manual:

Before using your air fryer for the first time, thoroughly read the manufacturer's manual. This will provide specific instructions and safety information tailored to your model. Understanding how your air fryer operates will help you use it correctly and safely.

Preheat Properly:

Always preheat your air fryer if the recipe calls for it. This step ensures that the appliance reaches the desired cooking temperature, helping to cook your food evenly. Most air fryers will beep when they are preheated and ready for use.

Avoid Overcrowding:

Overcrowding the basket can obstruct air circulation, resulting in uneven cooking and potentially causing the appliance to overheat. Cook food in batches if necessary, ensuring there is enough space for the hot air to circulate around each item.

Use Appropriate Cookware:

Only use the accessories and cookware recommended by the manufacturer. Metal utensils are generally safe, but avoid using plastic or non-stick utensils that could potentially damage the basket or release harmful chemicals.

Handle with Care:

The air fryer gets extremely hot during operation. Always use oven mitts or heat-resistant gloves when handling the basket or trays. Allow the appliance to cool down before cleaning or touching the interior.

Monitor Cooking Times:

While the air fryer is designed to be a set-and-forget appliance, it's important to keep an eye on cooking times, especially when trying new recipes. If your model doesn't have an automatic shut-off feature, set a timer to remind yourself to check the food regularly.

Keep the Air Fryer Clean:

Regularly clean the basket, tray, and interior to prevent the build-up of grease and food particles, which can pose a fire hazard. Use a damp cloth or sponge to wipe down the exterior of the appliance. Ensure all removable parts are thoroughly dried before reassembling them.

Avoid Using Oil Sprays with Aerosols:

If you need to use oil to achieve a crispy texture, opt for a refillable oil sprayer instead of aerosol sprays. Aerosol sprays can damage the non-stick coating of the air fryer basket and may also pose a fire risk.

Place on a Stable Surface:

Always place the air fryer on a flat, stable surface away from the edge of the counter. This helps prevent accidental tipping and ensures proper ventilation.

Be Aware of Steam:

When removing the basket or tray, be cautious of hot steam that can escape. Open the basket slowly to release the steam gradually and avoid burns.

By adhering to these safety tips, you'll ensure a safer cooking environment and enjoy the benefits of air frying with confidence.

EXCLUSIVE BONUS

40 Weight Loss Recipes

&

14 Days Meal Plan

Scan the QR-Code and receive
the FREE download:

CHAPTER 1:
MORNING DELIGHTS AND BRUNCH CLASSICS (20 RECIPES)

FULL ENGLISH BREAKFAST IN A FLASH

Servings: 2 | Difficulty: Easy | Temperature: 180°C |
Preparation Time: 10 minutes | Cooking Time: 20 minutes

INGREDIENTS:

- 4 rashers of bacon (100g)
- 4 sausages (200g)
- 2 eggs
- 2 tomatoes, halved (200g)
- 150g mushrooms, sliced
- 200g baked beans
- 4 slices of bread
- 1 tbsp vegetable oil
- Salt and pepper to taste

NUTRITION FACTS PER 100G:
Energy: 170 kcal | Protein: 8.5g | Total Fat: 10g | Saturated Fat: 3g |
Carbohydrates: 12g | Sugars: 2g | Dietary Fibre: 2g |

PREPARATION:

1. Preheat the air fryer to 180°C for 5 minutes.
2. Place the bacon rashers and sausages in the air fryer basket. Ensure they are not overlapping.
3. Set the air fryer timer for 10 minutes and cook, flipping halfway through for even browning.
4. After 10 minutes, remove the bacon and sausages and set aside, keeping them warm.
5. Place tomatoes, cut side up, and mushrooms in the air fryer basket. Drizzle with vegetable oil and season with salt and pepper.
6. Cook the vegetables for 5 minutes at 180°C.
7. Lightly toast the bread in the air fryer for 2-3 minutes or until golden brown.
8. While the bread is toasting, crack the eggs into small ramekins or air fryer-safe dishes.
9. Place the ramekins in the air fryer and cook for 4-5 minutes, or until the eggs reach your desired doneness.
10. Warm the baked beans in a microwave or on the stovetop until heated through.
11. Arrange everything on a plate: bacon, sausages, eggs, tomatoes, mushrooms, baked beans, and toasted bread. Serve immediately for a hearty, traditional breakfast.

CRISPY HASH BROWN BITES

Servings: 4 | Difficulty: Easy | Temperature: 200°C |
Preparation Time: 15 minutes | Cooking Time: 15 minutes

INGREDIENTS:

- 500g potatoes, peeled and grated
- 1 small onion, finely chopped
- 1 egg, beaten
- 50g plain flour
- 1 tsp salt
- 1/2 tsp black pepper
- 1/2 tsp garlic powder
- 2 tbsp vegetable oil

NUTRITION FACTS PER 100G:
Energy: 122 kcal | Protein: 2.5g | Total Fat: 5g | Saturated Fat: 0.7g |
Carbohydrates: 16g | Sugars: 1.2g | Dietary Fibre: 1.5g |

PREPARATION:

1. Begin by thoroughly washing the potatoes after peeling. Grate the potatoes using a box grater or food processor, then place them in a clean kitchen towel and squeeze out as much excess liquid as possible.
2. In a large mixing bowl, combine the grated potatoes with the finely chopped onion. Stir in the beaten egg until the mixture is well combined.
3. Next, add the plain flour, salt, black pepper, and garlic powder to the potato mixture. Mix everything together until evenly distributed.
4. Preheat your air fryer to 200°C for about 5 minutes to ensure it's at the perfect temperature for cooking.
5. Form the mixture into small, bite-sized patties, making sure they are all approximately the same size for even cooking.
6. Lightly brush each hash brown bite with vegetable oil to help achieve a crispy exterior.
7. Arrange the patties in a single layer in the air fryer basket, ensuring they don't overlap to allow hot air to circulate around them.
8. Cook the hash brown bites in the preheated air fryer for approximately 15 minutes, flipping them halfway through the cooking time to ensure they are golden brown and crispy on all sides.
9. Once cooked, carefully remove the crispy hash brown bites from the air fryer and transfer them to a serving plate.

AIR FRYER SCOTCH PANCAKES

Servings: 4 | Difficulty: Easy | Temperature: 180°C |
Preparation Time: 10 minutes | Cooking Time: 8 minutes

INGREDIENTS:

- 200g self-raising flour
- 50g caster sugar
- 1 tsp baking powder
- 1/4 tsp salt
- 250ml whole milk
- 1 large egg
- 1 tsp vanilla extract
- 25g unsalted butter, melted
- cooking spray or a little extra melted butter for greasing
- maple syrup or honey for serving (optional)

NUTRITION FACTS PER 100G:
Energy: 250 kcal | Protein: 5g | Total Fat: 8g | Saturated Fat: 4g |
Carbohydrates: 35g | Sugars: 10g | Dietary Fibre: 1g |

PREPARATION:

1. Begin by preheating your air fryer to 180°C. This step ensures your air fryer is ready for cooking as soon as the batter is mixed.
2. In a large mixing bowl, combine the self-raising flour, caster sugar, baking powder, and salt. Use a whisk to mix them thoroughly, ensuring all the dry ingredients are well incorporated.
3. In another bowl, whisk together the whole milk, large egg, vanilla extract, and melted butter. They should blend into a smooth, homogenous mixture.
4. Pour the wet ingredients into the bowl with the dry ingredients. Stir gently until the batter is smooth and there are no lumps. Be careful not to over mix, as this could make the pancakes tough.
5. Lightly grease the air fryer basket with cooking spray or a bit of melted butter to prevent sticking. Spoon in dollops of batter, ensuring they have enough space to spread and cook evenly.
6. Place the basket in the preheated air fryer and cook the pancakes at 180°C for 4 minutes. Check them halfway through to ensure they are cooking evenly. If needed, you can flip them gently with a spatula.
7. Once golden brown and cooked through (you can check with a toothpick—if it comes out clean, they are done), carefully remove the pancakes from the air fryer.
8. Serve the Scotch pancakes warm, drizzled with maple syrup or honey if desired.

GOLDEN CROISSANTS WITH CHEDDAR AND HAM

Servings: 4 | Difficulty: Easy | Temperature: 180°C |
Preparation Time: 15 minutes | Cooking Time: 10 minutes

INGREDIENTS:

- 4 ready-made croissant dough sheets (approx. 320g)
- 100g cheddar cheese, grated
- 100g ham, thinly sliced
- 1 egg, beaten (for egg wash)
- 1 tbsp dijon mustard (optional)

NUTRITION FACTS PER 100G:
Energy: 315 kcal | Protein: 10g | Total Fat: 20g | Saturated Fat: 10g |
Carbohydrates: 22g | Sugars: 2g | Dietary Fibre: 1g |

PREPARATION:

1. Begin by unrolling the croissant dough sheets and dividing them into triangles if not pre-divided. Ensure the perforations are sealed if any are broken.
2. If using, spread a light layer of dijon mustard on each triangle.
3. Place a slice of ham on each dough triangle, making sure it's within the edges to avoid spillage.
4. Sprinkle a generous amount of grated cheddar cheese over the ham.
5. Starting from the base, carefully roll each dough triangle toward the tip to form a croissant shape. Press the edges gently to seal.
6. Lightly brush each croissant with the beaten egg to achieve a golden brown finish.
7. Preheat your air fryer to 180°C for about 3 minutes to ensure even cooking.
8. Arrange the croissants in the air fryer basket, ensuring they are not touching to allow proper air circulation.
9. Cook the croissants in the air fryer at 180°C for 8-10 minutes until they are puffed up and golden brown.
10. Once cooked, remove the croissants from the air fryer and allow them to cool slightly before serving.

HERBED MUSHROOM AND SPINACH FRITTATA

Servings: 4 | Difficulty: Easy | Temperature: 180°C |
Preparation Time: 15 minutes | Cooking Time: 20 minutes

INGREDIENTS:

- 200g mushrooms, sliced
- 100g fresh spinach, washed and chopped
- 6 large eggs
- 100ml milk
- 50g grated cheddar cheese
- 2 tbsp olive oil
- 1 small onion, finely chopped
- 2 cloves garlic, minced
- 1 tsp dried thyme
- 1 tsp dried oregano
- salt and pepper, to taste

NUTRITION FACTS PER 100G:
Energy: 108 kcal | Protein: 7g | Total Fat: 8g | Saturated Fat: 2.5g |
Carbohydrates: 2.5g | Sugars: 1g | Dietary Fibre: 1g |

PREPARATION:

1. Begin by preheating the air fryer to 180°C.
2. Heat 1 tablespoon of olive oil in a frying pan over medium heat. Add the finely chopped onion and cook until soft and translucent, which should take around 3-4 minutes.
3. Introduce the minced garlic to the pan and cook for an additional minute until fragrant.
4. Add the sliced mushrooms to the pan and sauté until they are softened and have released their moisture, approximately 5 minutes.
5. Stir in the fresh spinach and cook until wilted, then season with dried thyme, dried oregano, salt, and pepper. Remove the mixture from the heat and set aside.
6. In a mixing bowl, whisk together the eggs and milk until well combined. Add the grated cheddar cheese and stir.
7. Lightly grease a baking dish that fits into your air fryer using the remaining tablespoon of olive oil. Pour the mushroom and spinach mixture evenly into the dish.
8. Pour the egg mixture over the vegetables, making sure it distributes evenly.
9. Carefully place the baking dish into the preheated air fryer and cook for 20 minutes, or until the frittata is set and golden on top.
10. Allow the frittata to cool slightly before slicing. Serve warm and enjoy.

AIR FRYER POACHED EGGS ON AVOCADO TOAST

Servings: 2 | Difficulty: Medium | Temperature: 180°C |
Preparation Time: 10 minutes | Cooking Time: 5 minutes

INGREDIENTS:

- 4 large eggs
- 2 ripe avocados
- 2 slices of wholegrain bread
- 1 tbsp lemon juice
- 1/4 tsp sea salt
- 1/4 tsp black pepper
- 1/4 tsp crushed red pepper flakes
- 10ml white vinegar
- fresh coriander leaves, for garnish

NUTRITION FACTS PER 100G:
Energy: 180 kcal | Protein: 6g | Total Fat: 14g | Saturated Fat: 3g |
Carbohydrates: 10g | Sugars: 1g | Dietary Fibre: 5g |

PREPARATION:

1. First, prepare the avocados by slicing them in half, removing the stone, and scooping the flesh into a bowl.
2. Mash the avocado with a fork until it reaches your desired consistency.
3. Add lemon juice, sea salt and black pepper to the mashed avocado and mix well.
4. Toast the slices of wholegrain bread in the air fryer at 180°C for 3-4 minutes, until golden and crispy.
5. Meanwhile, take two ramekins and pour 5ml of white vinegar into each.
6. Crack an egg into each ramekin, making sure the yolk remains intact.
7. Carefully place the ramekins into the air fryer basket and cook at 180°C for 5 minutes.
8. While the eggs are poaching, spread the prepared avocado mixture generously over each slice of toasted bread.
9. Once the eggs are done, carefully remove them from the ramekins and place them on top of the avocado-topped toast.
10. Sprinkle with crushed red pepper flakes and garnish with fresh coriander leaves.

CINNAMON FRENCH TOAST STICKS

Servings: 4 | Difficulty: Easy | Temperature: 180°C |
Preparation Time: 10 minutes | Cooking Time: 10 minutes

INGREDIENTS:

- 4 slices of thick white bread
- 2 large eggs
- 60ml whole milk
- 1 tsp vanilla extract
- 1 tsp ground cinnamon
- 50g granulated sugar
- 30g unsalted butter, melted
- maple syrup, for serving

NUTRITION FACTS PER 100G:
Energy: 245 kcal | Protein: 6g | Total Fat: 11g | Saturated Fat: 5g |
Carbohydrates: 30g | Sugars: 12g | Dietary Fibre: 1g |

PREPARATION:

1. Begin by cutting each slice of thick white bread into three equal sticks. This will give you a total of 12 sticks.
2. In a large bowl, whisk together the eggs, whole milk, and vanilla extract until well combined.
3. In a shallow dish, mix the ground cinnamon and granulated sugar; set aside.
4. Next, dip each bread stick into the egg mixture, ensuring it is fully coated. Allow any excess to drip off.
5. Coat the air fryer basket with a light layer of melted butter using a brush or non-stick spray.
6. Arrange the coated bread sticks in a single layer in the air fryer basket, making sure they do not touch each other.
7. Cook at 180°C for approximately 8-10 minutes, flipping halfway through to ensure they are evenly crisped and golden brown.
8. Once cooked, immediately remove the French toast sticks from the air fryer and roll them in the cinnamon sugar mixture until thoroughly coated.
9. Serve warm with a drizzle of maple syrup and enjoy!

CRISPY BACON BUTTIES

Servings: 4 | Difficulty: Easy | Temperature: 200°C |
Preparation Time: 10 minutes | Cooking Time: 12 minutes

INGREDIENTS:

- 8 rashers of streaky bacon
- 4 soft white rolls
- 50g butter, softened
- 4 tbsp tomato ketchup
- 4 tsp brown sauce
- 100g mixed salad leaves

NUTRITION FACTS PER 100G:
Energy: 250 kcal | Protein: 8g | Total Fat: 15g | Saturated Fat: 6g |
Carbohydrates: 20g | Sugars: 4g | Dietary Fibre: 2g |

PREPARATION:

1. Preheat the air fryer to 200°C for about 5 minutes.
2. Arrange the rashers of streaky bacon in a single layer in the air fryer basket, ensuring they do not overlap.
3. Cook the bacon in the air fryer for 10-12 minutes, turning halfway through, until it becomes crispy and golden.
4. While the bacon is cooking, slice the soft white rolls open and spread the softened butter evenly on the inner sides of each roll.
5. Once the bacon is done, carefully remove it from the air fryer and let it rest on a plate lined with kitchen paper to absorb any excess fat.
6. Place two rashers of crispy bacon on each buttered roll.
7. Top each bacon rasher with 1 tablespoon of tomato ketchup and 1 teaspoon of brown sauce.
8. Add a handful of mixed salad leaves to each roll for a fresh crunch and additional flavour.
9. Close the rolls and press them gently to hold everything in place.
10. Serve the crispy bacon butties immediately while they are still warm and enjoy.

FLUFFY AIR FRYER SCONES WITH CLOTTED CREAM

Servings: 6 | Difficulty: Medium | Temperature: 180°C |
Preparation Time: 15 minutes | Cooking Time: 12 minutes

INGREDIENTS:

- 250g self-raising flour
- 50g unsalted butter, cold and cubed
- 25g caster sugar
- 1 large egg
- 100ml whole milk
- a pinch of salt
- 1 tsp baking powder
- extra flour for dusting
- clotted cream, to serve
- strawberry jam, to serve

NUTRITION FACTS PER 100G:
Energy: 295 kcal | Protein: 6.5g | Total Fat: 10g | Saturated Fat: 6g |
Carbohydrates: 40g | Sugars: 10g | Dietary Fibre: 1g |

PREPARATION:

1. Begin by sifting the self-raising flour, baking powder, and salt into a large mixing bowl.
2. Add the cold, cubed butter to the bowl and, using your fingertips, rub the butter into the flour mixture until it resembles fine breadcrumbs.
3. Stir in the caster sugar, ensuring it's evenly distributed.
4. Crack the egg into a measuring jug and lightly beat it. Top up with whole milk until you reach 100ml of liquid in total. Combine well.
5. Create a well in the centre of the dry ingredients and pour in the egg and milk mixture. Mix gently with a knife or spatula until a soft dough forms.
6. Lightly flour a clean surface and turn the dough out onto it. Knead very briefly to bring it together until smooth.
7. Roll the dough to a thickness of about 2.5 cm. Using a floured cutter, cut out scones and place them on a piece of parchment paper suitable for the air fryer.
8. Preheat your air fryer to 180°C for a few minutes.
9. Carefully place the parchment paper with the scones into the air fryer basket.
10. Air fry the scones for 10-12 minutes, or until they have risen and are golden brown on top.
11. Once cooked, remove the scones and allow them to cool slightly on a wire rack.

SMOKY SAUSAGE ROLLS

Servings: 8 | Difficulty: Easy | Temperature: 180°C |
Preparation Time: 15 minutes | Cooking Time: 15 minutes

INGREDIENTS:

- 400g sausage meat
- 1 tsp smoked paprika
- 1 tsp dried thyme
- 1 tsp Dijon mustard
- 1 egg, beaten
- 1 sheet ready-rolled puff pastry (approximately 275g)
- salt and pepper to taste
- 1 tbsp sesame seeds (optional)

NUTRITION FACTS PER 100G:
Energy: 317 kcal | Protein: 8.5g | Total Fat: 23g | Saturated Fat: 10g |
Carbohydrates: 18g | Sugars: 0.8g | Dietary Fibre: 1g |

PREPARATION:

1. Begin by preheating the air fryer to 180°C and line the basket with parchment paper.
2. In a large bowl, combine the sausage meat, smoked paprika, dried thyme, and Dijon mustard. Mix thoroughly until all ingredients are well incorporated. Season with salt and pepper to taste.
3. Unroll the puff pastry sheet onto a lightly floured surface and cut it in half lengthwise to create two long rectangles.
4. Divide the sausage mixture into two equal portions and shape each portion into a long sausage shape, placing one along the centre of each puff pastry rectangle.
5. Brush the edges of the pastry with some of the beaten egg. Fold the pastry over the sausage filling, pressing the edges to seal and create a roll. Ensure the seam is on the bottom.
6. Cut each long roll into 4 equal pieces to make 8 sausage rolls in total.
7. Lay the sausage rolls seam-side down in the air fryer basket, leaving space between each one. Brush the tops with the remaining beaten egg.
8. Optionally, sprinkle sesame seeds over the tops of the sausage rolls for added texture and flavour.
9. Air fry the sausage rolls at 180°C for 12-15 minutes, or until they are golden brown and the pastry is cooked through.
10. Carefully remove the sausage rolls from the air fryer and allow them to cool slightly on a wire rack before serving.

SWEET POTATO BREAKFAST HASH

Servings: 4 | Difficulty: Easy | Temperature: 200°C |
Preparation Time: 10 minutes | Cooking Time: 20 minutes

INGREDIENTS:

- 500g sweet potatoes, peeled and diced
- 1 red bell pepper, diced
- 1 small red onion, finely chopped
- 2 tbsp olive oil
- 1 tsp smoked paprika
- 1 tsp ground cumin
- 1/2 tsp garlic powder
- salt and pepper, to taste
- 4 large eggs
- fresh coriander leaves, chopped, for garnish

NUTRITION FACTS PER 100G:
Energy: 115 kcal | Protein: 2.5g | Total Fat: 7g | Saturated Fat: 1.5g |
Carbohydrates: 10g | Sugars: 3g | Dietary Fibre: 2g

PREPARATION:

1. Start by preheating the air fryer to 200°C.
2. In a large bowl, combine the diced sweet potatoes, red bell pepper, and chopped red onion.
3. Next, drizzle the olive oil over the vegetables and toss well to ensure they're evenly coated.
4. Sprinkle the smoked paprika, ground cumin, garlic powder, salt, and pepper over the mixture. Again, toss to combine, ensuring the spices are well-distributed.
5. Transfer the seasoned vegetable mix to the air fryer basket, spreading them out in an even layer.
6. Cook in the preheated air fryer for 15 minutes, shaking the basket halfway through to ensure even cooking.
7. After 15 minutes, create four small wells in the hash and crack an egg into each well.
8. Return the basket to the air fryer and cook for an additional 5 minutes or until the eggs are cooked to your liking.
9. Remove from the air fryer and transfer the hash to serving plates.
10. Finally, garnish with chopped fresh coriander leaves and serve immediately.

AIR FRYER GRANOLA CLUSTERS

Servings: 6 | Difficulty: Easy | Temperature: 160°C |
Preparation Time: 10 minutes | Cooking Time: 15 minutes

INGREDIENTS:

- 200g rolled oats
- 50g chopped almonds
- 50g sunflower seeds
- 50g dried cranberries
- 75ml honey
- 3 tbsp coconut oil, melted
- 1 tsp vanilla extract
- 1/2 tsp ground cinnamon
- pinch of sea salt

NUTRITION FACTS PER 100G:
Energy: 450 kcal | Protein: 8g | Total Fat: 20g | Saturated Fat: 8g |
Carbohydrates: 57g | Sugars: 18g | Dietary Fibre: 8g |

PREPARATION:

1. Begin by mixing the rolled oats, chopped almonds, sunflower seeds, and dried cranberries in a large bowl. Ensure the mixture is well combined.
2. In a separate small bowl, whisk together the honey, melted coconut oil, vanilla extract, ground cinnamon, and a pinch of sea salt until smooth.
3. Pour the honey mixture over the oat mixture, stirring with a spatula to evenly coat all the dry ingredients.
4. Preheat the air fryer to 160°C for 3 minutes.
5. Line the air fryer basket with a piece of baking paper. This will prevent sticking and make it easier to remove the granola clusters once cooked.
6. Gently spread the granola mixture in an even layer on the baking paper. Aim for uniform thickness to ensure even cooking.
7. Place the basket in the air fryer and cook for 15 minutes, shaking the basket halfway through to ensure even cooking.
8. Once golden and slightly crisp, remove the basket from the air fryer and allow the granola clusters to cool completely in the basket. This will help them firm up and become crunchy.
9. After they have cooled, break the granola into clusters of your desired size. Store in an airtight container at room temperature for up to a week.

BLACK PUDDING AND APPLE BREAKFAST BITES

Servings: 4 | Difficulty: Medium | Temperature: 180°C |
Preparation Time: 10 minutes | Cooking Time: 15 minutes

INGREDIENTS:

- 200g black pudding, cut into small chunks
- 1 large cooking apple, peeled, cored, and diced
- 1 small onion, finely chopped
- 1 tbsp olive oil
- 50g breadcrumbs
- 1 tsp dried thyme
- 25g butter, melted
- salt and pepper to taste

NUTRITION FACTS PER 100G:
Energy: 250 kcal | Protein: 8g | Total Fat: 15g | Saturated Fat: 6g |
Carbohydrates: 20g | Sugars: 5g | Dietary Fibre: 2g |

PREPARATION:

1. Begin by preheating your air fryer to 180°C.
2. In a medium frying pan, heat the olive oil over medium heat. Add the chopped onion and cook until softened, approximately 5 minutes.
3. Combine the diced apple with the onion in the frying pan, stirring occasionally until the apple softens, about 3 minutes.
4. Transfer the onion and apple mixture to a large bowl. Add the chunks of black pudding, breadcrumbs, dried thyme, melted butter, salt, and pepper.
5. Mix everything thoroughly until well-combined. Form the mixture into bite-sized balls, making sure each bite is firmly packed.
6. Lightly grease the air fryer basket with a little olive oil to prevent sticking.
7. Arrange the breakfast bites in the air fryer basket in a single layer, ensuring they are not touching each other.
8. Air fry the black pudding and apple bites at 180°C for 15 minutes, shaking the basket halfway through the cooking time to ensure even crisping.
9. Once cooked and golden brown, carefully remove the bites from the air fryer and let them cool for a few minutes before serving.
10. Serve warm and enjoy your delicious Black Pudding and Apple Breakfast Bites.

CHEESE AND CHIVE SAVOURY MUFFINS

Servings: 6 | Difficulty: Easy | Temperature: 180°C |
Preparation Time: 15 mins | Cooking Time: 15 mins

INGREDIENTS:

- 150g self-raising flour
- 100g cheddar cheese, grated
- 100ml whole milk
- 50g unsalted butter, melted
- 2 large eggs
- 3 tbsp chives, finely chopped
- 1/2 tsp salt
- 1/2 tsp black pepper

NUTRITION FACTS PER 100G:
Energy: 253 kcal | Protein: 9.7g | Total Fat: 15.7g | Saturated Fat: 8.9g |
Carbohydrates: 17.7g | Sugars: 1.1g | Dietary Fibre: 0.7g |

PREPARATION:

1. Start by preheating your air fryer to 180°C.
2. In a large mixing bowl, combine the self-raising flour, grated cheddar cheese, chopped chives, salt, and black pepper.
3. In a separate bowl, whisk together the whole milk, melted butter, and eggs until well combined.
4. Carefully pour the wet ingredients into the dry ingredients, stirring gently until just mixed. Be careful not to over mix.
5. Spoon the batter evenly into silicone muffin cups, filling each about three-quarters full.
6. Gently place the filled muffin cups into the air fryer basket, ensuring they are not touching to allow for even cooking.
7. Cook the muffins in the air fryer at 180°C for 12-15 minutes, or until a skewer inserted into the centre comes out clean and the tops are golden brown.
8. Once cooked, remove the muffins from the air fryer and allow them to cool in the muffin cups for a few minutes before transferring to a wire rack to cool completely.

AIR-FRIED SHAKSHUKA CUPS

Servings: 6 | Difficulty: Medium | Temperature: 180°C |
Preparation Time: 15 minutes | Cooking Time: 20 minutes

INGREDIENTS:

- 1 tbsp olive oil
- 1 small onion, finely chopped (about 80g)
- 1 red bell pepper, diced (about 150g)
- 2 cloves garlic, minced
- 400g canned chopped tomatoes
- 1 tsp ground cumin
- 1 tsp paprika
- 1/2 tsp ground coriander
- salt and pepper to taste
- 6 large eggs
- fresh parsley or coriander, chopped, for garnish
- 100g feta cheese, crumbled
- 6 puff pastry squares (10cm x 10cm)

NUTRITION FACTS PER 100G:
Energy: 165 kcal | Protein: 4.5g | Total Fat: 11g | Saturated Fat: 3.5g |
Carbohydrates: 12g | Sugars: 3g | Dietary Fibre: 1.7g |

PREPARATION:

1. Begin by preheating your air fryer to 180°C.
2. In a medium frying pan, warm the olive oil over medium heat.
3. Add finely chopped onion and diced red bell pepper. Sauté until they become soft, about 5 minutes.
4. Incorporate the minced garlic, cooking for an additional minute until fragrant.
5. Pour in the canned chopped tomatoes, stirring to combine.
6. Sprinkle the mixture with ground cumin, paprika, and ground coriander. Add salt and pepper to taste.
7. Reduce the heat and let the sauce simmer for 10 minutes, allowing the flavours to meld together.
8. While the sauce simmers, prepare the puff pastry squares by placing them in individual silicone muffin cups. Ensure the pastry slightly overhangs the edges of the cups.
9. Evenly distribute the tomato-pepper mixture into each prepared puff pastry cup.
10. Crack one egg on top of the shakshuka mixture in each cup, taking care not to break the yolk.
11. Carefully place the muffin cups into the preheated air fryer basket.
12. Air-fry the shakshuka cups at 180°C for about 10-12 minutes, or until the puff pastry is golden and the egg whites are set but yolks are still runny.
13. Once cooked, remove the shakshuka cups from the air fryer and let them cool slightly.
14. Garnish each cup with crumbled feta cheese and a sprinkling of fresh parsley or coriander.
15. Serve the shakshuka cups warm and enjoy your delightful, airy creation.

BLUEBERRY OAT BREAKFAST BARS

Servings: 8 | Difficulty: Easy | Temperature: 180°C |
Preparation Time: 15 minutes | Cooking Time: 20 minutes

INGREDIENTS:

- 150g rolled oats
- 100g almond flour
- 50g desiccated coconut
- 50g brown sugar
- 1 tsp baking powder
- 1/2 tsp ground cinnamon
- 1/4 tsp salt
- 120ml maple syrup
- 1 tbsp coconut oil, melted
- 1 large egg, beaten
- 1 tsp vanilla extract
- 150g fresh blueberries

NUTRITION FACTS PER 100G:
Energy: 358 kcal | Protein: 6.5g | Total Fat: 14g | Saturated Fat: 5g |
Carbohydrates: 51g | Sugars: 18g | Dietary Fibre: 6g |

PREPARATION:

1. Begin by preheating your air fryer to 180°C.
2. In a large mixing bowl, combine the rolled oats, almond flour, desiccated coconut, brown sugar, baking powder, ground cinnamon, and salt. Mix all the dry ingredients thoroughly.
3. In a separate bowl, whisk together the maple syrup, melted coconut oil, beaten egg, and vanilla extract until well blended.
4. Gradually pour the wet mixture into the dry ingredients, stirring constantly to ensure everything is well incorporated.
5. Gently fold in the fresh blueberries, taking care not to squish them too much.
6. Line a suitable air fryer baking dish with parchment paper.
7. Pour the blueberry oat mixture into the prepared baking dish, spreading it out evenly and pressing it down lightly with a spatula.
8. Place the baking dish in the preheated air fryer and cook for 20 minutes, or until the bars are golden brown and firm to the touch.
9. Once cooked, remove the baking dish from the air fryer and let it cool completely.
10. After cooling, cut into 8 bars and enjoy your freshly made Blueberry Oat Breakfast Bars.

QUICK AND EASY AIR FRYER OMELETTE

Servings: 2 | Difficulty: Easy | Temperature: 180°C |
Preparation Time: 10 minutes | Cooking Time: 15 minutes

INGREDIENTS:

- 4 large eggs
- 50g cheddar cheese, grated
- 50ml milk
- 1 small red onion, finely chopped
- 1 small red bell pepper, diced
- 50g cherry tomatoes, halved
- 1 tbsp olive oil
- salt and pepper, to taste
- fresh parsley, chopped (for garnish)

NUTRITION FACTS PER 100G:
Energy: 168 kcal | Protein: 9g | Total Fat: 12g | Saturated Fat: 4g |
Carbohydrates: 4g | Sugars: 2g | Dietary Fibre: 1g |

PREPARATION:

1. Begin by cracking the eggs into a mixing bowl. Add the milk and a pinch of salt and pepper. Whisk everything together until well combined and slightly frothy.
2. Prepare the vegetables by finely chopping the red onion, dicing the red bell pepper, and halving the cherry tomatoes.
3. In a small pan, heat the olive oil over medium heat. Sauté the red onion and bell pepper until softened, which should take about 5 minutes. Set aside to cool slightly.
4. Preheat your air fryer to 180°C. While the air fryer is heating up, mix the sautéed vegetables into the egg mixture.
5. Grease two small, oven-safe dishes or ramekins with a little bit of olive oil. Divide the egg and vegetable mixture evenly between the two dishes.
6. Sprinkle the grated cheddar cheese over the top of each dish. Place the dishes carefully into the air fryer basket.
7. Cook for 10-15 minutes, or until the omelettes are fully set and the cheese is golden and bubbly.
8. Once done, remove the dishes from the air fryer using oven mitts as they will be hot. Let them cool for a minute or two.
9. Garnish with freshly chopped parsley before serving.

BUTTERY CRUMPETS WITH HONEYCOMB

Servings: 4 | Difficulty: Medium | Temperature: 180°C |
Preparation Time: 20 minutes + 1 hour rising time | Cooking Time: 10 minutes

INGREDIENTS:

- 250g strong white bread flour
- 1 tsp salt
- 1 tbsp sugar
- 1 tsp instant yeast
- 200ml warm milk
- 100ml warm water
- 50g melted butter
- honeycomb pieces for serving

NUTRITION FACTS PER 100G:
Energy: 230 kcal | Protein: 6g | Total Fat: 6g | Saturated Fat: 3g |
Carbohydrates: 36g | Sugars: 5g | Dietary Fibre: 2g |

PREPARATION:

1. Start by combining the flour and salt in a large mixing bowl. In a separate bowl, mix together the sugar and yeast with the warm milk, allowing it to sit for a few minutes until it becomes frothy.
2. Gradually pour the wet ingredients into the dry ingredients, stirring continuously with a wooden spoon. Slowly add the warm water, mixing until you achieve a smooth batter.
3. Cover the bowl with a clean tea towel and leave the batter to rise in a warm place for about 1 hour, or until it has doubled in size and has lots of bubbles on the surface.
4. After the batter has risen, preheat your air fryer to 180°C. Lightly grease crumpet rings and place them in the air fryer basket.
5. Spoon the batter into each crumpet ring, filling them about halfway full. Cook in the air fryer for approximately 5 minutes until the crumpets are set and the tops are dry and full of holes.
6. Carefully remove the crumpets from the rings, flip them over, and continue cooking for another 3-5 minutes until they are golden brown and cooked through.
7. Once cooked, immediately brush the crumpets with the melted butter while they are still hot. This will give them a rich, buttery flavour.
8. Serve the crumpets warm, topped with delicious chunks of honeycomb and an extra drizzle of honey if desired.

BREAKFAST BEAN BURRITOS

Servings: 4 | Difficulty: Easy | Temperature: 180°C |
Preparation Time: 15 minutes | Cooking Time: 12 minutes

INGREDIENTS:

- 200g canned black beans, drained and rinsed
- 100g cheddar cheese, grated
- 4 large flour tortillas
- 4 large eggs
- 1 small red onion, finely chopped
- 1 red pepper, diced
- 1 tsp olive oil
- 1 tsp ground cumin
- 1 tsp smoked paprika
- 50ml milk
- salt and pepper, to taste
- fresh coriander, chopped, for garnish
- salsa, for serving

NUTRITION FACTS PER 100G:
Energy: 170 kcal | Protein: 7g | Total Fat: 8g | Saturated Fat: 3g |
Carbohydrates: 16g | Sugars: 2g | Dietary Fibre: 3g |

PREPARATION:

1. Begin by heating the olive oil in a frying pan over medium heat. Sauté the red onion and red pepper until they have softened, usually around 5 minutes.
2. In a mixing bowl, whisk together the eggs, milk, cumin, and smoked paprika. Season with salt and pepper to taste.
3. Pour the egg mixture into the pan with the softened vegetables. Stir constantly to scramble the eggs until they are fully cooked, about 5-7 minutes. Remove from heat.
4. Lay out the flour tortillas on a clean surface. Divide the scrambled egg mixture evenly among the tortillas, placing it in the centre of each one.
5. Evenly distribute the black beans and grated cheddar cheese on top of the scrambled eggs in each tortilla.
6. Carefully roll up each tortilla, folding in the sides first, then rolling from the bottom to encase the filling fully.
7. Preheat your air fryer to 180°C. Once preheated, place the burritos in the basket, seam-side down, to keep them from unrolling. Depending on the size of your air fryer, you may need to cook in batches.
8. Cook the burritos for approximately 6 minutes. Open the air fryer, carefully flip each burrito, and continue cooking for an additional 6 minutes, or until the tortillas are golden brown and crispy.
9. Remove the burritos from the air fryer and allow them to cool for a few minutes before serving.
10. Garnish the burritos with freshly chopped coriander and serve with a side of salsa.

PORRIDGE TOPPED WITH ROASTED NUTS

Servings: 2 | Difficulty: Easy | Temperature: 180°C |
Preparation Time: 10 minutes | Cooking Time: 25 minutes

INGREDIENTS:

- 100g porridge oats
- 500ml whole milk
- 200ml water
- 1 tsp vanilla extract
- 1 tbsp honey

- 50g mixed nuts
- 1 tbsp sunflower oil
- 1 tsp ground cinnamon
- fresh fruits (optional)

NUTRITION FACTS PER 100G:
Energy: 180 kcal | Protein: 4g | Total Fat: 7g | Saturated Fat: 2g |
Carbohydrates: 24g | Sugars: 7g | Dietary Fibre: 3g |

PREPARATION:

1. Combine the porridge oats, whole milk, and water in an oven-safe dish that fits into your air fryer basket.
2. Mix in the vanilla extract and honey, ensuring the ingredients are well combined.
3. Preheat the air fryer to 180°C.
4. Once preheated, place the dish in the air fryer and set the timer for 20 minutes. Stir halfway through to ensure the porridge cooks evenly.
5. While the porridge is cooking, prepare the roasted nuts. Toss the mixed nuts in a bowl with sunflower oil and ground cinnamon until they are evenly coated.
6. After 20 minutes, carefully remove the porridge dish using oven mitts. Give it a good stir.
7. Place the seasoned nuts directly into the air fryer basket and cook for 5 minutes at 180°C, shaking the basket halfway through to ensure even roasting.
8. Once done, take the nuts out and allow them to cool slightly. They should be crispy and aromatic.
9. Serve the porridge in bowls and generously sprinkle the roasted nuts on top.
10. Optionally, you can add fresh fruits for an extra burst of flavour and nutrition.

CHAPTER 2:
LIGHT BITES AND APPETIZERS
(20 RECIPES)

GARLIC AND ROSEMARY POTATO WEDGES

Servings: 4 | Difficulty: Easy | Temperature: 200°C |
Preparation Time: 10 minutes | Cooking Time: 25 minutes

INGREDIENTS:

- 600g potatoes, washed and cut into wedges
- 2 tbsp olive oil
- 3 garlic cloves, minced
- 1 tbsp fresh rosemary, finely chopped
- 1 tsp sea salt
- 1/2 tsp black pepper

NUTRITION FACTS PER 100G:
Energy: 120 kcal | Protein: 2g | Total Fat: 5g | Saturated Fat: 0.8g |
Carbohydrates: 17g | Sugars: 1g | Dietary Fibre: 2g |

PREPARATION:

1. Preheat the air fryer to 200°C.
2. Place the potato wedges in a large bowl. Drizzle with olive oil, ensuring they are evenly coated.
3. Sprinkle the minced garlic, chopped rosemary, sea salt, and black pepper over the potatoes. Toss well to distribute the seasoning.
4. Arrange the seasoned potato wedges in the air fryer basket in a single layer, making sure they are not overlapping.
5. Cook the wedges for 20-25 minutes, shaking the basket halfway through to ensure even cooking.
6. Check for doneness by inserting a fork into the potatoes; they should be tender inside and crispy outside.
7. Once cooked, remove the potato wedges from the air fryer and let them cool for a few minutes before serving.

CRISPY CAULIFLOWER BUFFALO BITES

Servings: 4 | Difficulty: Easy | Temperature: 190°C |
Preparation Time: 15 minutes | Cooking Time: 20 minutes

INGREDIENTS:

- 500g cauliflower florets
- 120g plain flour
- 240ml milk
- 1 tsp garlic powder
- 1 tsp onion powder
- 1 tsp smoked paprika
- 1/2 tsp salt
- 1/2 tsp black pepper
- 100ml hot sauce
- 60g unsalted butter, melted
- 2 tbsp chopped fresh parsley (optional, for garnish)

NUTRITION FACTS PER 100G:
Energy: 130 kcal | Protein: 3.5g | Total Fat: 6.5g | Saturated Fat: 3.5g |
Carbohydrates: 14g | Sugars: 2g | Dietary Fibre: 2g |

PREPARATION:

1. Begin by preheating your air fryer to 190°C.
2. In a mixing bowl, combine the flour, garlic powder, onion powder, smoked paprika, salt, and black pepper.
3. Gradually add the milk to the dry ingredients, stirring until a smooth batter forms.
4. Dip each cauliflower floret into the batter, ensuring they are evenly coated.
5. Place the coated cauliflower florets in a single layer in the air fryer basket. Avoid overcrowding for best results.
6. Air fry the cauliflower bites at 190°C for 15 minutes, shaking the basket halfway through to ensure even cooking.
7. While the cauliflower is cooking, in a separate bowl, mix the hot sauce with the melted butter until well combined.
8. Once the cauliflower bites are done, transfer them to a large bowl. Pour the hot sauce mixture over the cauliflower and toss to coat thoroughly.
9. Return the cauliflower bites to the air fryer and cook for an additional 5 minutes to crisp up.
10. After cooking, remove the cauliflower bites from the air fryer and transfer them to a serving platter. Garnish with chopped parsley if desired.

PANKO-CRUSTED MOZZARELLA STICKS

Servings: 4 | Difficulty: Easy | Temperature: 200°C |
Preparation Time: 15 minutes | Cooking Time: 8 minutes

INGREDIENTS:

- 200g mozzarella cheese, cut into sticks
- 60g plain flour
- 2 large eggs, beaten
- 120g panko breadcrumbs
- 1 tsp dried oregano
- 1 tsp dried basil
- 1/2 tsp garlic powder
- 1/4 tsp salt
- 1/4 tsp black pepper
- cooking spray

NUTRITION FACTS PER 100G:
Energy: 270 kcal | Protein: 16g | Total Fat: 14g | Saturated Fat: 7g |
Carbohydrates: 23g | Sugars: 1g | Dietary Fibre: 1g |

PREPARATION:

1. Begin by setting up your dredging station: place the flour in one bowl, the beaten eggs in another, and the panko breadcrumbs combined with dried oregano, dried basil, garlic powder, salt, and black pepper in a third bowl.
2. Roll each mozzarella stick first in the flour, ensuring it is fully coated. Shake off any excess flour and dip it into the beaten eggs, allowing any surplus egg to drip off.
3. Finally, roll the egg-coated cheese stick in the panko mixture, pressing lightly to adhere the breadcrumbs thoroughly to the surface. Repeat for all sticks and arrange them on a plate.
4. Lightly spray the mozzarella sticks with cooking spray, ensuring a light and even coating which helps achieve a golden, crispy texture.
5. Preheat your air fryer to 200°C for about 5 minutes.
6. Once preheated, arrange the mozzarella sticks in a single layer in the air fryer basket, being careful not to overcrowd them to ensure even cooking.
7. Air fry the sticks at 200°C for 6-8 minutes, turning them halfway through the cooking time to ensure they are crisped evenly on all sides. They are done when the coating is golden brown and the cheese is melted and gooey.
8. Serve the panko-crusted mozzarella sticks immediately, with your favourite dipping sauce for a deliciously crunchy and cheesy snack.

MINI FISHCAKES WITH TARTARE DIP

Servings: 4 | Difficulty: Easy | Temperature: 180°C |
Preparation Time: 20 minutes | Cooking Time: 12 minutes

INGREDIENTS:

- 200g boneless white fish fillets (e.g., cod or haddock)
- 100g potatoes, peeled and boiled
- 1 tbsp fresh parsley, finely chopped
- 1 tsp Dijon mustard
- 1 small onion, finely chopped
- 1 clove garlic, minced
- 1 egg, beaten
- 50g breadcrumbs
- salt and black pepper, to taste
- 50g plain flour
- 2 tbsp olive oil (for brushing)
- 100g mayonnaise
- 1 tbsp capers, finely chopped
- 1 tbsp gherkins, finely chopped
- 1 tsp lemon juice
- fresh dill, for garnish (optional)

NUTRITION FACTS PER 100G:
Energy: 185 kcal | Protein: 12g | Total Fat: 10g | Saturated Fat: 1.5g |
Carbohydrates: 14g | Sugars: 1g | Dietary Fibre: 1g |

PREPARATION:

1. Start by flaking the cooked fish fillets into a large mixing bowl, ensuring there are no remaining bones.
2. Mash the boiled potatoes with a fork and add them to the fish.
3. Stir in the chopped parsley, Dijon mustard, onion, and minced garlic.
4. Season the mixture generously with salt and black pepper, then add the beaten egg and breadcrumbs. Mix well until all ingredients are fully combined.
5. Using your hands, shape the fish mixture into small, round cakes, approximately 2 inches in diameter.
6. Roll each fishcake lightly in plain flour, shaking off any excess.
7. Preheat your air fryer to 180°C.
8. Before cooking, gently brush each fishcake with a small amount of olive oil to help them crisp up in the air fryer.
9. Arrange the fishcakes in a single layer in the air fryer basket, ensuring they are not touching. You may need to cook them in batches.
10. Air-fry the fishcakes for 10-12 minutes, turning halfway through the cooking time, until they are golden brown and crispy.
11. While the fishcakes are cooking, prepare the tartare dip by mixing the mayonnaise, chopped capers, gherkins, and lemon juice in a small bowl.
12. To serve, place the hot, crispy fishcakes on a serving platter with the tartare dip on the side. Garnish with fresh dill if desired.

STICKY HONEY-SOY CHICKEN BREAST BITES

Servings: 4 | Difficulty: Easy | Temperature: 180°C |
Preparation Time: 15 minutes | Cooking Time: 20 minutes

INGREDIENTS:

- 500g chicken breast, cut into bite-sized pieces
- 60ml honey
- 60ml soy sauce
- 1 tbsp rice vinegar
- 1 tbsp sesame oil
- 2 cloves garlic, minced
- 1 tsp fresh ginger, grated
- 1 tbsp cornflour
- salt and pepper to taste
- 1 tbsp sesame seeds (optional)
- fresh coriander for garnish

NUTRITION FACTS PER 100G:
Energy: 150 kcal | Protein: 15g | Total Fat: 5g | Saturated Fat: 1g |
Carbohydrates: 10g | Sugars: 8g | Dietary Fibre: 0.5g |

PREPARATION:

1. In a bowl, combine honey, soy sauce, rice vinegar, sesame oil, garlic, and ginger. Mix thoroughly.
2. Add the chicken breast pieces to the bowl, ensuring each piece is well coated with the sauce. Allow to marinate for at least 15 minutes.
3. Preheat your air fryer to 180°C.
4. Once marinated, lightly dust the chicken pieces with cornflour. This helps the sauce to adhere better and become sticky.
5. Place the chicken pieces in the air fryer basket in a single layer. Avoid overcrowding to ensure even cooking.
6. Air fry the chicken for around 15-20 minutes or until fully cooked, shaking the basket halfway through for even browning.
7. As the chicken is cooking, heat any remaining marinade in a small pan until it reduces to a thick glaze.
8. Once the chicken is done, toss it in the reduced glaze for an extra sticky coating.
9. Garnish with sesame seeds and fresh coriander before serving.

CRISP AIR FRYER FALAFEL BALLS

Servings: 4 | Difficulty: Medium | Temperature: 180°C |
Preparation Time: 15 minutes | Cooking Time: 15 minutes

INGREDIENTS:

- 400g canned chickpeas, drained and rinsed
- 1 small onion, finely chopped
- 4 cloves garlic, minced
- 15g fresh parsley, chopped
- 15g fresh coriander, chopped
- 1 tsp ground cumin
- 1 tsp ground coriander
- 1/2 tsp ground black pepper
- 1/2 tsp ground cayenne pepper
- 1 tsp baking powder
- 30g plain flour
- 2 tbsp olive oil
- Salt to taste

NUTRITION FACTS PER 100G:
Energy: 190 kcal | Protein: 6g | Total Fat: 6g | Saturated Fat: 1g |
Carbohydrates: 26g | Sugars: 2g | Dietary Fibre: 6g |

PREPARATION:

1. Begin by adding the chickpeas, chopped onion, and minced garlic into a food processor. Blend until the mixture is coarse.
2. Next, incorporate the fresh parsley and coriander, followed by the ground cumin, ground coriander, black pepper, and cayenne pepper. Pulse the mixture until well combined.
3. Transfer the mixture into a large bowl. Stir in the baking powder, plain flour, and salt. Knead the mixture until it forms a cohesive dough.
4. Shape the falafel mixture into small balls, roughly the size of a walnut. Aim to keep the balls uniform for even cooking.
5. Brush each falafel ball lightly with olive oil. Preheat the air fryer to 180°C.
6. Carefully place the falafel balls in the air fryer basket, ensuring they have some space between them for air circulation.
7. Air fry the falafel balls for 15 minutes, shaking the basket halfway through the cooking time to ensure they cook evenly and achieve a golden brown exterior.
8. Once cooked, remove the falafel balls from the air fryer. Allow them to cool slightly before serving.

BLACK PEPPER AND SEA SALT SQUID RINGS

Servings: 4 | Difficulty: Easy | Temperature: 180°C |
Preparation Time: 15 minutes | Cooking Time: 10 minutes

INGREDIENTS:

- 500g fresh squid rings
- 2 tbsp olive oil
- 1 tsp sea salt
- 1 tsp freshly ground black pepper
- 2 garlic cloves, finely chopped
- 1 tsp smoked paprika
- 1 lemon, cut into wedges (for serving)
- fresh parsley, chopped (for garnish)

NUTRITION FACTS PER 100G:
Energy: 120 kcal | Protein: 15g | Total Fat: 5g | Saturated Fat: 0.8g |
Carbohydrates: 3g | Sugars: 0.5g | Dietary Fibre: 1g |

PREPARATION:

1. Begin by preheating your air fryer to 180°C.
2. In a large mixing bowl, combine the olive oil, sea salt, freshly ground black pepper, finely chopped garlic, and smoked paprika.
3. Toss the fresh squid rings in the bowl, ensuring each ring is evenly coated with the seasoning mixture.
4. Arrange the seasoned squid rings in a single layer in the air fryer basket to allow consistent cooking.
5. Cook the squid rings at 180°C for 10 minutes, shaking the basket halfway through the cooking time to ensure even crispness.
6. Once cooking is complete, carefully place the air-fried squid rings onto a serving platter.
7. Garnish with chopped fresh parsley and serve immediately with lemon wedges on the side.

SWEET CHILLI HALLOUMI FRIES

Servings: 4 | Difficulty: Easy | Temperature: 180°C |
Preparation Time: 10 minutes | Cooking Time: 10 minutes

INGREDIENTS:

- 250g halloumi cheese
- 60g plain flour
- 1 tsp smoked paprika
- 1 tsp garlic powder
- 1/2 tsp black pepper
- 1/2 tsp cayenne pepper
- 2 tbsp vegetable oil
- 3 tbsp sweet chilli sauce
- fresh coriander leaves, chopped (for garnish)

NUTRITION FACTS PER 100G:
Energy: 268 kcal | Protein: 10g | Total Fat: 18g | Saturated Fat: 8g |
Carbohydrates: 15g | Sugars: 6g | Dietary Fibre: 1g |

PREPARATION:

1. Begin by preheating the air fryer to 180°C.
2. Slice the halloumi into thick, even sticks resembling fries.
3. In a shallow dish, combine the plain flour, smoked paprika, garlic powder, black pepper, and cayenne pepper.
4. Dredge each halloumi stick in the seasoned flour mixture, ensuring an even coating.
5. Lightly brush or spray the halloumi sticks with the vegetable oil.
6. Carefully arrange the halloumi fries in the air fryer basket, ensuring they do not touch.
7. Cook the halloumi fries in the air fryer for 8-10 minutes, turning them halfway through for an even crisp.
8. While the fries are cooking, warm the sweet chilli sauce in a small saucepan over a low heat.
9. Once the halloumi fries are golden and crispy, remove them from the air fryer and place on a serving plate.
10. Drizzle the warm sweet chilli sauce generously over the fries.
11. Garnish with freshly chopped coriander leaves.

CRISPY VEGETABLE PAKORAS

Servings: 4 | Difficulty: Medium | Temperature: 180°C |
Preparation Time: 20 minutes | Cooking Time: 15 minutes

INGREDIENTS:

- 200g gram flour (chickpea flour)
- 100ml water
- 1 tsp salt
- 1 tsp turmeric powder
- 1 tsp ground coriander
- 1 tsp ground cumin
- 1/2 tsp chilli powder
- 1/2 tsp baking soda
- 1 small onion, thinly sliced
- 100g spinach leaves, chopped
- 100g aubergine, diced
- 1 small potato, grated
- 1 green chilli, finely chopped
- 2 tbsp coriander leaves, finely chopped
- 1 tbsp lemon juice
- cooking spray

NUTRITION FACTS PER 100G:
Energy: 140 kcal | Protein: 6.5g | Total Fat: 3.5g | Saturated Fat: 0.7g |
Carbohydrates: 20g | Sugars: 3g | Dietary Fibre: 5g |

PREPARATION:

1. Begin by combining the gram flour, salt, turmeric powder, ground coriander, ground cumin, chilli powder, and baking soda in a large mixing bowl.
2. Gradually add the water while stirring continuously to create a smooth, lump-free batter.
3. Stir the thinly sliced onion into the batter, ensuring it is well-coated.
4. Follow by adding the chopped spinach leaves, diced aubergine, and grated potato. Mix thoroughly to combine.
5. Include the finely chopped green chilli and coriander leaves to the mixture. Integrate these ingredients well.
6. Add lemon juice to the batter, blending it into the mixture until evenly distributed.
7. Preheat the air fryer to 180°C for about 5 minutes.
8. Lightly grease the air fryer basket with cooking spray to prevent sticking.
9. Scoop small portions of the vegetable mixture and shape them into rough balls or patties.
10. Arrange the pakoras in a single layer in the air fryer basket, making sure they do not touch each other.
11. Lightly spray the tops with cooking spray for extra crispiness.
12. Cook the pakoras at 180°C for 15 minutes, turning them halfway through the cooking time for even browning.
13. Once golden brown and crispy, remove the pakoras from the air fryer and let them cool slightly on a wire rack.
14. Serve hot with your favourite chutney or dipping sauce.

PARMESAN COURGETTE FRIES

Servings: 4 | Difficulty: Easy | Temperature: 200°C |
Preparation Time: 15 minutes | Cooking Time: 12 minutes

INGREDIENTS:

- 2 medium courgettes (about 300g), cut into fries
- 50g grated Parmesan cheese
- 50g breadcrumbs
- 1 tbsp dried mixed herbs
- 1 tsp garlic powder
- 1/2 tsp salt
- 1/4 tsp black pepper
- 2 tbsp plain flour
- 1 large egg, beaten
- cooking spray or a small amount of olive oil

NUTRITION FACTS PER 100G:
Energy: 125 kcal | Protein: 7g | Total Fat: 5g | Saturated Fat: 2g |
Carbohydrates: 12g | Sugars: 2g | Dietary Fibre: 2g |

PREPARATION:

1. Begin by preheating your air fryer to 200°C to ensure it's ready for cooking.
2. Simultaneously, grab a medium bowl and combine the Parmesan cheese, breadcrumbs, dried mixed herbs, garlic powder, salt, and black pepper.
3. Next, take another bowl and add the plain flour. This will assist in giving the courgette fries a light coating before dredging.
4. In a third bowl, beat the large egg, creating an egg wash for the fries.
5. Start by dipping each courgette fry into the plain flour, coating it lightly, then immerse it into the beaten egg.
6. Once the courgettes are covered in the egg, proceed to roll them in the Parmesan and breadcrumb mixture, ensuring an even coverage.
7. After all fries are coated, arrange them in a single layer in the air fryer basket. Avoid overcrowding to promote even cooking.
8. Lightly spray the courgette fries with cooking spray or brush them with a small amount of olive oil to help them achieve a crispy texture.
9. Cook the fries in the preheated air fryer for about 12 minutes, flipping them halfway through, until they are golden brown and crispy.
10. Once cooked, remove the fries from the air fryer, let them cool for a few minutes, and then serve immediately while they're still warm and crunchy.

AIR FRYER SCOTCH EGGS

Servings: 4 | Difficulty: Medium | Temperature: 180°C |
Preparation Time: 20 minutes | Cooking Time: 20 minutes

INGREDIENTS:

- 4 large eggs
- 200g sausage meat
- 50g plain flour
- 2 eggs, beaten
- 100g breadcrumbs
- 1 tsp mustard powder (optional)
- 1 tsp salt
- 1/2 tsp black pepper
- 1/2 tsp paprika
- cooking spray

NUTRITION FACTS PER 100G:
Energy: 250 kcal | Protein: 12g | Total Fat: 18g | Saturated Fat: 5g |
Carbohydrates: 12g | Sugars: 1g | Dietary Fibre: 1g |

PREPARATION:

1. Begin by boiling the eggs: Place the large eggs in a saucepan filled with water and bring to a boil. Once boiling, cook for 6 minutes for a slightly runny yolk or 8 minutes for a firmer yolk. Immediately transfer to a bowl of iced water to cool. Peel the eggs carefully once cooled.

2. In a mixing bowl, combine the sausage meat with mustard powder (if using), salt, black pepper, and paprika. Mix thoroughly to incorporate the seasonings.

3. Divide the sausage meat mixture into four equal portions. Flatten each portion into a patty. Wrap each egg with a sausage patty, ensuring it is completely sealed and evenly covered.

4. Set up three separate bowls: one with flour, one with beaten eggs, and one with breadcrumbs.

5. Coat each sausage-wrapped egg in flour first, shaking off any excess. Then dip it into the beaten eggs, allowing any excess to drip off. Finally, roll it in the breadcrumbs to cover completely.

6. Preheat your air fryer to 180°C for 3 minutes.

7. Lightly spray the basket of the air fryer with cooking spray to prevent sticking. Arrange the prepared Scotch eggs in the basket in a single layer. Lightly spray the tops of the Scotch eggs with cooking spray for an even, crispy finish.

8. Air fry the Scotch eggs at 180°C for 18–20 minutes or until the sausage meat is cooked through and the coating is golden brown and crispy. Turn them halfway through the cooking time for even browning.

9. Once cooked, carefully remove the Scotch eggs from the air fryer and let them rest for a few minutes before serving.

SMOKY BBQ PULLED PORK SLIDERS

Servings: 8 sliders | Difficulty: Moderate | Temperature: 180°C |
Preparation Time: 15 minutes | Cooking Time: 1 hour 30 minutes

INGREDIENTS:

- 700g pork shoulder
- 3 tbsp smoky BBQ sauce
- 1 tbsp olive oil
- 1 tsp smoked paprika
- 1 tsp garlic powder
- 1 tsp onion powder
- 1 tsp sea salt
- 1/2 tsp ground black pepper
- 120ml apple juice
- 8 brioche slider buns
- 150g coleslaw mix
- 2 tbsp mayonnaise
- 1 tbsp apple cider vinegar

NUTRITION FACTS PER 100G:
Energy: 250 kcal | Protein: 15g | Total Fat: 15g | Saturated Fat: 4g |
Carbohydrates: 15g | Sugars: 5g | Dietary Fibre: 1g |

PREPARATION:

1. Start by preheating your air fryer to 180°C.
2. Combine the smoked paprika, garlic powder, onion powder, sea salt, and ground black pepper in a small bowl.
3. Rub the pork shoulder with olive oil and then coat it evenly with the spice mixture.
4. Place the seasoned pork shoulder into the air fryer basket and pour the apple juice around it.
5. Cook the pork shoulder at 180°C for 1 hour and 30 minutes, flipping halfway through to ensure even cooking.
6. While the pork is cooking, prepare the coleslaw by mixing the coleslaw mix, mayonnaise, and apple cider vinegar in a bowl.
7. Once the pork is done, remove it from the air fryer and let it rest for 10 minutes.
8. After resting, shred the pork using two forks and mix in the smoky BBQ sauce until well combined.
9. Slice the brioche slider buns and lightly toast them in the air fryer for about 2-3 minutes.
10. Assemble the sliders by layering the pulled pork and coleslaw on the toasted buns.
11. Serve immediately and enjoy your smoky BBQ pulled pork sliders!

BREADED MUSHROOMS WITH GARLIC AIOLI

Servings: 4 | Difficulty: Easy | Temperature: 200°C |
Preparation Time: 15 minutes | Cooking Time: 10 minutes

INGREDIENTS:

- 400g button mushrooms, cleaned and stems trimmed
- 100g plain flour
- 2 eggs, beaten
- 100g breadcrumbs

- 50g grated Parmesan cheese
- 1 tsp dried oregano
- 1 tsp dried thyme
- 1 tsp garlic powder
- salt and pepper, to taste
- olive oil spray

For the Garlic Aioli:
- 100ml mayonnaise
- 1 tbsp lemon juice
- 2 garlic cloves, minced
- salt and pepper, to taste

NUTRITION FACTS PER 100G:
Energy: 166 kcal | Protein: 6.5g | Total Fat: 10.5g | Saturated Fat: 2.5g |
Carbohydrates: 12g | Sugars: 1.5g | Dietary Fibre: 1.5g |

PREPARATION:

1. Begin by preheating your air fryer to 200°C to ensure it's ready when you are.
2. In a medium bowl, mix the breadcrumbs, grated Parmesan cheese, dried oregano, dried thyme, garlic powder, salt, and pepper.
3. Place the plain flour in a shallow dish, and the beaten eggs in another.
4. Dredge each mushroom first in flour, shaking off any excess, then dip into the beaten eggs, ensuring it is fully coated.
5. Roll the egg-coated mushroom in the breadcrumb mixture, pressing lightly to adhere the coating evenly.
6. Arrange the breaded mushrooms in a single layer inside the air fryer basket, making sure they do not touch one another. Lightly spray with olive oil for extra crispiness.
7. Cook in the air fryer for 10 minutes, or until golden brown and crispy, shaking the basket halfway through the cooking time to ensure even cooking.
8. While the mushrooms are cooking, prepare the garlic aioli by mixing the mayonnaise, lemon juice, and minced garlic in a small bowl. Season with salt and pepper according to taste.
9. Transfer the mushrooms to a serving platter once they are done, and serve immediately alongside the prepared garlic aioli.

SWEETCORN AND CHILLI FRITTERS

Servings: 4 | Difficulty: Easy | Temperature: 180°C |
Preparation Time: 15 minutes | Cooking Time: 12 minutes

INGREDIENTS:

- 200g sweetcorn kernels (fresh or tinned, drained)
- 1 small red chilli, finely chopped
- 1 small red onion, finely chopped
- 100g self-raising flour
- 2 large eggs
- 50ml milk
- 1 tsp ground cumin
- 1 tsp smoked paprika
- 2 tbsp chopped fresh coriander
- salt and pepper to taste
- olive oil spray

NUTRITION FACTS PER 100G:
Energy: 150 kcal | Protein: 6g | Total Fat: 5g | Saturated Fat: 1g |
Carbohydrates: 18g | Sugars: 3g | Dietary Fibre: 2g |

PREPARATION:

1. Begin by placing the sweetcorn kernels, chopped red chilli, and chopped red onion into a large mixing bowl.
2. Next, sift in the self-raising flour, ensuring an even distribution throughout the mixture.
3. In another bowl, whisk the eggs and milk together until combined, and then add this to the sweetcorn mixture.
4. Season the batter with cumin, smoked paprika, chopped fresh coriander, and a pinch of salt and pepper.
5. Stir all the ingredients together until you achieve a smooth and consistent batter.
6. Preheat your air fryer to 180°C for about 3 minutes.
7. Lightly spray the air fryer basket with olive oil to prevent the fritters from sticking.
8. Using a tablespoon, drop spoonfuls of the batter into the air fryer basket, spacing them apart to allow for even cooking.
9. Air fry the fritters at 180°C for 6 minutes, then carefully flip them over and continue cooking for another 6 minutes, or until golden brown and crispy.
10. Once cooked, remove the fritters from the air fryer and place them on a paper towel-lined plate to remove any excess oil.
11. Serve the sweetcorn and chilli fritters hot, garnished with additional fresh coriander if desired.

AIR-FRIED ONION BHAJIS

Servings: 4 | Difficulty: Moderate | Temperature: 180°C |
Preparation Time: 15 minutes | Cooking Time: 12 minutes

INGREDIENTS:

- 200g gram flour (chickpea flour)
- 2 large onions, finely sliced
- 2 tbsp fresh coriander, chopped
- 1 tsp ground cumin
- 1 tsp ground coriander
- 1 tsp turmeric powder
- 1 tsp garam masala
- 1 tsp red chilli powder
- 1 tsp salt
- 1 tsp baking powder
- 100ml water
- 2 tbsp vegetable oil

NUTRITION FACTS PER 100G:
Energy: 145 kcal | Protein: 6.5g | Total Fat: 4.3g | Saturated Fat: 0.5g |
Carbohydrates: 21.5g | Sugars: 3.0g | Dietary Fibre: 4.1g |

PREPARATION:

1. Begin by slicing the onions finely and setting them aside in a large mixing bowl.
2. In a separate bowl, sift together the gram flour, ground cumin, ground coriander, turmeric powder, garam masala, red chilli powder, salt, and baking powder to ensure an even mixture.
3. Gradually add water to the dry ingredients, stirring continuously until a smooth and thick batter forms.
4. Incorporate the sliced onions and chopped fresh coriander into the batter, ensuring each onion slice is well coated.
5. Preheat the air fryer to 180°C.
6. Lightly brush or spray the air fryer basket with a bit of vegetable oil to prevent sticking.
7. Using your hands or a spoon, shape portions of the onion mixture into small, uneven fritters, and carefully place them in the air fryer basket, ensuring they do not touch.
8. Drizzle the remaining vegetable oil over the bhajis.
9. Air fry the bhajis for 12 minutes, turning them halfway through the cooking time to achieve an even, golden brown crispness.
10. Once cooked, remove the bhajis from the air fryer and place them on a plate lined with kitchen paper to drain any excess oil.
11. Serve the hot onion bhajis immediately with your favourite chutney or dipping sauce.

BUTTERMILK FRIED CHICKEN TENDERS

Servings: 4 | Difficulty: Medium | Temperature: 200°C |
Preparation Time: 20 minutes (plus 2 hours marinating time) | Cooking Time: 15 minutes

INGREDIENTS:

- 500g chicken breast tenders
- 250ml buttermilk
- 2 large eggs
- 100g plain flour
- 100g breadcrumbs
- 1 tsp garlic powder
- 1 tsp onion powder
- 1 tsp paprika
- 1 tsp salt
- 1/2 tsp black pepper
- 1/2 tsp cayenne pepper (optional for extra heat)
- 1 tbsp olive oil or cooking spray

NUTRITION FACTS PER 100G:
Energy: 165 kcal | Protein: 18g | Total Fat: 5g | Saturated Fat: 1g |
Carbohydrates: 13g | Sugars: 1g | Dietary Fibre: 1g |

PREPARATION:

1. Begin by marinating the chicken tenders. In a large bowl, mix the chicken tenders with the buttermilk until they are well-coated. Cover the bowl and refrigerate for at least 2 hours to allow the buttermilk to tenderize the chicken.
2. After marinating, prepare the breading stations. In one shallow dish, beat the eggs. In a second shallow dish, combine the plain flour, garlic powder, onion powder, paprika, salt, black pepper, and cayenne pepper, mixing well. In a third dish, place the breadcrumbs.
3. Dip each chicken tender into the flour mixture, ensuring they are entirely coated. Then, dip them into the beaten eggs, followed by a coating in the breadcrumbs. Press slightly to ensure the breadcrumbs adhere well.
4. Preheat your air fryer to 200°C for about 3 minutes.
5. Lightly spray the air fryer basket with olive oil or cooking spray to prevent sticking. Arrange the breaded chicken tenders in a single layer in the basket, ensuring they do not overlap.
6. Air fry the chicken tenders at 200°C for 10-15 minutes, turning them halfway through the cooking process to ensure they are evenly cooked and golden brown on both sides.
7. Once cooked, remove the chicken tenders from the air fryer and let them rest for a couple of minutes before serving.

BACON-WRAPPED JALAPEÑO POPPERS

Servings: 4 | Difficulty: Easy | Temperature: 180°C |
Preparation Time: 15 minutes | Cooking Time: 12 minutes

INGREDIENTS:

- 12 large jalapeños
- 200g cream cheese
- 100g cheddar cheese, grated
- 1 tsp garlic powder
- 1 tsp onion powder
- 12 slices streaky bacon
- 1 tbsp olive oil
- salt and pepper to taste

NUTRITION FACTS PER 100G:
Energy: 240 kcal | Protein: 8g | Total Fat: 20g | Saturated Fat: 10g |
Carbohydrates: 4g | Sugars: 2g | Dietary Fibre: 1g |

PREPARATION:

1. Begin by washing the jalapeños thoroughly. To prepare them, slice each jalapeño in half lengthwise and remove the seeds and membranes.
2. In a mixing bowl, combine the cream cheese, cheddar cheese, garlic powder, onion powder, salt, and pepper. Mix until all ingredients are well-blended and the texture is creamy.
3. With great care, fill each jalapeño half with the cream cheese mixture using a small spoon.
4. Next, take a slice of streaky bacon and wrap it around each stuffed jalapeño half, ensuring the cheese filling is securely enclosed. Use a toothpick to hold the bacon in place if necessary.
5. Lightly brush each bacon-wrapped jalapeño popper with olive oil to enhance crispiness during cooking.
6. Preheat your air fryer to 180°C. Arrange the jalapeño poppers in the air fryer basket, making sure they are not overcrowded to allow even cooking.
7. Cook the jalapeño poppers for 12 minutes, turning them halfway through to ensure the bacon is evenly crispy and the cheese filling is bubbly.
8. Once done, carefully remove the jalapeño poppers from the air fryer and allow them to cool slightly before serving.

AIR FRYER SAUSAGE AND APPLE BITES

Servings: 4 | Difficulty: Easy | Temperature: 180°C |
Preparation Time: 10 minutes | Cooking Time: 15 minutes

INGREDIENTS:

- 250g pork sausages
- 2 medium apples, cored and diced
- 1 small red onion, finely chopped
- 1 tbsp olive oil
- 1 tsp dried sage
- 1 tsp dried thyme
- 1 tbsp honey
- salt and pepper, to taste

> **NUTRITION FACTS PER 100G:**
> Energy: 185 kcal | Protein: 7g | Total Fat: 12g | Saturated Fat: 4g |
> Carbohydrates: 12g | Sugars: 10g | Dietary Fibre: 1g |

PREPARATION:

1. Begin by cutting the pork sausages into bite-sized pieces. Make sure they are evenly sized for uniform cooking.
2. In a large mixing bowl, combine the diced apples, finely chopped red onion, and sausage pieces.
3. Drizzle the olive oil over the mixture, ensuring all ingredients are lightly coated.
4. Sprinkle the dried sage, dried thyme, salt, and pepper over the mixture. Toss everything together until well combined.
5. Preheat your air fryer to 180°C for about 3 minutes to ensure it is hot enough for cooking.
6. Arrange the sausage and apple mixture in a single layer in the air fryer basket. Do not overcrowd; if necessary, cook in batches.
7. Allow the mixture to cook for 10 minutes, shaking the basket halfway through to ensure even cooking.
8. After 10 minutes, drizzle the honey over the top and cook for an additional 5 minutes, or until the sausages are cooked through and the apples are tender.
9. Remove the sausage and apple bites from the air fryer and serve immediately, garnished with a sprinkle of fresh herbs if desired.

CHEDDAR-STUFFED JALAPEÑO PEPPERS

Servings: 4 | Difficulty: Easy | Temperature: 190°C |
Preparation Time: 15 minutes | Cooking Time: 10 minutes

INGREDIENTS:

- 8 large jalapeño peppers (about 120g)
- 100g cheddar cheese, grated
- 50g cream cheese, softened
- 1 garlic clove, minced
- 1 spring onion, finely chopped
- 30g breadcrumbs
- 1 tbsp olive oil
- salt and pepper to taste

NUTRITION FACTS PER 100G:
Energy: 230 kcal | Protein: 7.5g | Total Fat: 18g | Saturated Fat: 8g |
Carbohydrates: 8g | Sugars: 2g | Dietary Fibre: 2g |

PREPARATION:

1. Begin by washing the jalapeño peppers thoroughly. Using a small knife, slit each pepper lengthwise and carefully remove seeds and membranes to reduce the heat.
2. Set aside the jalapeños and focus on preparing the filling. In a medium-sized mixing bowl, blend together the grated cheddar cheese, softened cream cheese, minced garlic, and chopped spring onion until well combined.
3. Season the cheese mixture with salt and pepper to your preference, ensuring an even distribution of seasoning.
4. Using a spoon or piping bag, stuff each jalapeño pepper with the cheese mixture, making sure they are generously filled but not overstuffed.
5. In a small bowl, mix the breadcrumbs with the olive oil to moisten them slightly. Gently press a layer of the breadcrumb mixture on top of the stuffed peppers for an extra crunch.
6. Preheat your air fryer to 190°C. Meanwhile, arrange the stuffed jalapeños in a single layer in the air fryer basket, ensuring they do not overlap.
7. Cook the jalapeño peppers in the preheated air fryer for 8-10 minutes, or until the peppers are tender and the breadcrumbs are golden and crisp.
8. Carefully remove the peppers from the air fryer and allow them to cool for a couple of minutes before serving.

AIR-FRIED VEGETABLE SPRING ROLLS

Servings: 12 spring rolls | Difficulty: Medium | Temperature: 190°C |
Preparation Time: 25 minutes | Cooking Time: 15 minutes

INGREDIENTS:

- 200g cabbage, finely shredded
- 100g carrots, julienned
- 100g bean sprouts
- 1 red bell pepper, thinly sliced
- 2 spring onions, finely chopped
- 2 cloves garlic, minced
- 1 tsp grated fresh ginger
- 2 tbsp soy sauce
- 1 tbsp sesame oil
- 12 spring roll wrappers
- 1 tbsp cornflour mixed with 2 tbsp water (for sealing)
- cooking spray

NUTRITION FACTS PER 100G:
Energy: 80 kcal | Protein: 2.2g | Total Fat: 3.2g | Saturated Fat: 0.5g |
Carbohydrates: 11g | Sugars: 3.2g | Dietary Fibre: 2g |

PREPARATION:

1. Begin by preparing the filling. In a large bowl, mix the shredded cabbage, julienned carrots, bean sprouts, red bell pepper, and spring onions.
2. Next, in a small pan over medium heat, heat the sesame oil and add the minced garlic and grated ginger. Sauté for about 1 minute until fragrant.
3. Add the soy sauce to the pan, stir well, and cook for an additional 2 minutes.
4. Pour the warm mixture over the vegetable blend and toss to combine thoroughly. Let the filling cool for a few minutes.
5. To assemble the spring rolls, place a wrapper on a clean surface with one corner pointing towards you. Spoon about 2 tablespoons of the vegetable filling onto the bottom third of the wrapper.
6. Fold the bottom corner over the filling, then fold in the sides, and roll up tightly. Seal the edge with the cornflour mixture. Repeat with the remaining wrappers and filling.
7. Lightly brush or spray each spring roll with cooking spray to ensure crispiness without excess oil.
8. Preheat your air fryer to 190°C. Arrange the spring rolls in a single layer in the air fryer basket, ensuring they do not touch or overlap.
9. Air-fry the spring rolls for 10-15 minutes, turning them halfway through the cooking time, until they are golden brown and crispy.
10. Once cooked, remove the spring rolls from the air fryer and allow them to cool slightly before serving.
11. Serve the spring rolls hot with your favourite dipping sauce and enjoy their crunchy, flavourful goodness.

CHAPTER 3: SEAFOOD AND POULTRY CREATIONS (20 RECIPES)

LEMON AND HERB SALMON FILLETS

Servings: 2 | Difficulty: Easy | Temperature: 180°C |
Preparation Time: 10 minutes | Cooking Time: 12 minutes

INGREDIENTS:

- 2 salmon fillets (approx. 150g each)
- 1 lemon
- 2 tbsp olive oil
- 1 tsp dried thyme
- 1 tsp dried rosemary
- 1 tsp dried parsley
- 2 cloves garlic, minced
- salt and pepper, to taste

NUTRITION FACTS PER 100G:
Energy: 190 kcal | Protein: 19g | Total Fat: 13g | Saturated Fat: 2g |
Carbohydrates: 1g | Sugars: 0g | Dietary Fibre: 0.5g |

PREPARATION:

1. Begin by preheating the air fryer to 180°C.
2. While the air fryer is heating, zest the lemon and then cut it in half to extract the juice into a small bowl.
3. Incorporate the olive oil, dried thyme, rosemary, parsley, and minced garlic with the lemon juice and zest, then whisk together until well combined.
4. Rinse the salmon fillets under cold water and pat them dry with kitchen paper.
5. Place the salmon fillets in a shallow dish and pour the lemon and herb mixture over them, ensuring they are evenly coated. Let them marinate for 5 minutes.
6. Arrange the salmon fillets in the air fryer basket, making sure they are not overlapping.
7. Air fry the fillets for 12 minutes, checking halfway through to ensure they are cooking evenly.
8. Once the salmon is cooked through and flakes easily with a fork, remove from the air fryer.
9. Season the fillets with salt and pepper to taste.
10. Finally, serve the lemon and herb salmon fillets immediately with your favourite sides.

CRISPY BREADED COD

Servings: 4 | Difficulty: Easy | Temperature: 180°C |
Preparation Time: 15 minutes | Cooking Time: 15 minutes

INGREDIENTS:

- 4 cod fillets (approximately 150g each)
- 100g breadcrumbs
- 50g plain flour
- 2 large eggs
- 2 tbsp olive oil
- 1 tsp garlic powder
- 1 tsp paprika
- salt and pepper to taste
- lemon wedges (optional, for serving)

NUTRITION FACTS PER 100G:
Energy: 200 kcal | Protein: 18g | Total Fat: 7g | Saturated Fat: 1g |
Carbohydrates: 18g | Sugars: 1g | Dietary Fibre: 1g |

PREPARATION:

1. Start by preheating your air fryer to 180°C.
2. Next, prepare three separate bowls: fill the first with plain flour, the second with beaten eggs, and the third with seasoned breadcrumbs (mix breadcrumbs with garlic powder, paprika, salt, and pepper).
3. Pat the cod fillets dry with kitchen paper to remove excess moisture.
4. Coat each fillet in flour, shaking off any excess, then dip in the beaten eggs, ensuring they are fully covered.
5. Evenly cover the fillets with the seasoned breadcrumbs, pressing gently to adhere the coating.
6. Lightly drizzle or spray the olive oil over the breaded fillets to enhance crispiness.
7. Place the fillets in the air fryer basket, making sure they are not overcrowded.
8. Cook for 12-15 minutes, turning halfway through, until the fillets are golden brown and cooked through.
9. Serve immediately with lemon wedges on the side if desired.

THAI-STYLE KING PRAWNS

Servings: 4 | Difficulty: Medium | Temperature: 200°C |
Preparation Time: 15 minutes | Cooking Time: 10 minutes

INGREDIENTS:

- 500g king prawns, peeled and deveined
- 2 tbsp olive oil
- 3 cloves garlic, minced
- 1 red chilli, finely chopped
- 1 tbsp fish sauce
- 2 tbsp lime juice
- 1 tsp brown sugar
- 2 tbsp fresh coriander, chopped
- 1 tsp ground turmeric
- 1 tsp paprika
- salt, to taste
- black pepper, to taste

NUTRITION FACTS PER 100G:
Energy: 120 kcal | Protein: 15g | Total Fat: 6g | Saturated Fat: 1g |
Carbohydrates: 5g | Sugars: 1g | Dietary Fibre: 1g |

PREPARATION:

1. Begin by whisking together the olive oil, minced garlic, red chilli, fish sauce, lime juice, and brown sugar in a large bowl.
2. Introduce the king prawns to the marinade, ensuring they are well-coated. Let them marinate for at least 10 minutes.
3. In a small bowl, combine ground turmeric, paprika, salt, and black pepper.
4. Sprinkle the spice mixture over the marinated prawns and gently toss to coat evenly.
5. Prehcat thc air fryer to 200°C for about 3 minutes.
6. Arrange the seasoned prawns in a single layer in the air fryer basket.
7. Cook the prawns for 8-10 minutes, shaking the basket halfway through to ensure even cooking.
8. Finish by garnishing the cooked prawns with freshly chopped coriander.
9. Serve immediately with lime wedges if desired.

GARLIC BUTTER SCALLOPS

Servings: 2 | Difficulty: Easy | Temperature: 180°C |
Preparation Time: 10 minutes | Cooking Time: 8 minutes

INGREDIENTS:

◆ 300g scallops
◆ 50g unsalted butter, melted
◆ 2 cloves garlic, minced
◆ 1 tbsp lemon juice
◆ 1 tbsp fresh parsley, chopped
◆ salt, to taste
◆ black pepper, to taste

NUTRITION FACTS PER 100G:
Energy: 125 kcal | Protein: 10g | Total Fat: 8g | Saturated Fat: 4g |
Carbohydrates: 4g | Sugars: 0.5g | Dietary Fibre: 0.2g |

PREPARATION:

1. Begin by preheating the air fryer to 180°C.
2. Rinse the scallops under cold water and pat dry with kitchen paper. Season with salt and black pepper.
3. In a small bowl, combine the melted butter, minced garlic, and lemon juice.
4. Arrange the scallops in a single layer in the air fryer basket. Brush half of the garlic butter mixture over the scallops.
5. Air fry the scallops for 4 minutes.
6. Turn the scallops over, brushing the remaining garlic butter mixture on the other side.
7. Continue to air fry for another 4 minutes, or until the scallops are golden and cooked through.
8. Garnish with chopped fresh parsley before serving.

ROAST CHICKEN WITH SWEET AND SPICY GLAZE

Servings: 4 | Difficulty: Medium | Temperature: 180°C |
Preparation Time: 15 minutes | Cooking Time: 40 minutes

INGREDIENTS:

- 1 whole chicken (around 1.5kg)
- 2 tbsp olive oil
- 3 tbsp honey
- 2 tbsp soy sauce
- 1 tbsp sriracha sauce
- 1 tbsp lime juice
- 2 cloves garlic, minced
- 1 tsp paprika
- 1 tsp salt
- 1 tsp black pepper
- fresh coriander for garnish

NUTRITION FACTS PER 100G:
Energy: 190 kcal | Protein: 19g | Total Fat: 10g | Saturated Fat: 2.5g |
Carbohydrates: 4g | Sugars: 3g | Dietary Fibre: 0.4 g |

PREPARATION:

1. Preheat the air fryer to 180°C.
2. Pat the chicken dry with paper towels and rub it all over with olive oil.
3. In a small bowl, mix together the honey, soy sauce, sriracha sauce, lime juice, minced garlic, paprika, salt, and black pepper.
4. Generously coat the chicken with the prepared glaze, making sure to cover all areas evenly.
5. Place the chicken in the air fryer basket, breast side down.
6. Cook the chicken for 20 minutes.
7. Carefully turn the chicken over and cook for an additional 20 minutes, or until the internal temperature reaches 75°C and juices run clear.
8. Remove the chicken from the air fryer and let it rest for 10 minutes before carving.
9. Garnish with freshly chopped coriander before serving.

LEMON AND DILL HADDOCK FILLETS

Servings: 2 | Difficulty: Easy | Temperature: 180°C |
Preparation Time: 10 minutes | Cooking Time: 15 minutes

INGREDIENTS:

- 2 haddock fillets (approx. 300g total)
- 1 lemon
- 2 tbsp fresh dill, chopped
- 1 tbsp olive oil
- 1 garlic clove, minced
- salt, to taste
- black pepper, to taste
- 1 tbsp capers (optional)

NUTRITION FACTS PER 100G:
Energy: 110 kcal | Protein: 17g | Total Fat: 4g | Saturated Fat: 0.7g |
Carbohydrates: 1g | Sugars: 0.4g | Dietary Fibre: 0.5 g |

PREPARATION:

1. Start by preheating your air fryer to 180°C.
2. In a small bowl, combine the minced garlic, olive oil, salt, and black pepper. Mix well.
3. Pat the haddock fillets dry with paper towels.
4. Rub the garlic and oil mixture evenly over both sides of each haddock fillet.
5. Slice the lemon in half. Cut one half into thin slices and squeeze the juice from the other half.
6. Lay the lemon slices on top of each fillet, then sprinkle with chopped dill.
7. If using capers, scatter them over the fillets as well.
8. Place the prepared fish into the air fryer basket, ensuring the fillets are not overlapping.
9. Cook for 12-15 minutes, or until the fish is opaque and flakes easily with a fork.
10. Once cooking is complete, remove the fillets from the air fryer and drizzle with freshly squeezed lemon juice before serving.

CHICKEN FILLETS WITH SMOKED PAPRIKA

Servings: 4 | Difficulty: Easy | Temperature: 180°C |
Preparation Time: 10 minutes | Cooking Time: 20 minutes

INGREDIENTS:

- 4 chicken fillets (around 150g each)
- 2 tbsp olive oil
- 1 tbsp smoked paprika
- 1 tsp garlic powder
- 1 tsp onion powder
- 1 tsp dried thyme
- 1 tsp salt
- 1/2 tsp black pepper
- lemon wedges for serving (optional)

NUTRITION FACTS PER 100G:
Energy: 138 kcal | Protein: 20.5g | Total Fat: 4.8g | Saturated Fat: 0.8g |
Carbohydrates: 1.2g | Sugars: 0.3g | Dietary Fibre: 0.6g |

PREPARATION:

1. Start by preheating your air fryer to 180°C.
2. In a small bowl, combine olive oil, smoked paprika, garlic powder, onion powder, dried thyme, salt, and black pepper until well mixed.
3. Pat the chicken fillets dry with kitchen paper, then rub the spice mixture evenly over each fillet ensuring they are fully coated.
4. Place the seasoned chicken fillets in the air fryer basket, making sure they are not crowded. You may need to cook them in batches depending on the size of your air fryer.
5. Cook for 20 minutes, turning halfway through to ensure even cooking.
6. Once cooked, remove the chicken fillets from the air fryer and let them rest for a couple of minutes before serving.
7. Serve with lemon wedges if desired.

TANDOORI-SPICED CHICKEN PIECES

Servings: 4 | Difficulty: Medium | Temperature: 180°C |
Preparation Time: 15 minutes | Cooking Time: 20 minutes

INGREDIENTS:

- 500g chicken thighs, boneless and skinless
- 100ml Greek yoghurt
- 1 tbsp lemon juice
- 1 tbsp garlic paste
- 1 tbsp ginger paste
- 2 tsp ground coriander
- 2 tsp ground cumin
- 1 tsp ground turmeric
- 1 tsp paprika
- 1/2 tsp ground chilli powder
- 1 tbsp vegetable oil
- salt, to taste
- fresh coriander leaves, for garnish

NUTRITION FACTS PER 100G:
Energy: 150 kcal | Protein: 13g | Total Fat: 8g | Saturated Fat: 2g |
Carbohydrates: 5g | Sugars: 2g | Dietary Fibre: 1g |

PREPARATION:

1. Start by cutting the chicken thighs into medium-sized pieces.
2. In a large mixing bowl, combine the Greek yoghurt, lemon juice, garlic paste, and ginger paste.
3. Next, add the ground coriander, ground cumin, turmeric, paprika, chilli powder, vegetable oil, and salt. Mix thoroughly to form a marinade.
4. Immerse the chicken pieces into the yoghurt mixture, ensuring every piece is well-coated.
5. Allow the chicken to marinate for at least 1 hour in the refrigerator to absorb the flavours.
6. Preheat your air fryer to 180°C.
7. Lightly grease the air fryer basket with a bit of vegetable oil.
8. Place the marinated chicken pieces in a single layer in the air fryer basket, avoiding overcrowding.
9. Cook the chicken for 20 minutes, turning halfway through, until they are golden brown and fully cooked.
10. Garnish with freshly chopped coriander leaves before serving.

GARLIC AND PARMESAN PRAWNS

Servings: 4 | Difficulty: Easy | Temperature: 180°C |
Preparation Time: 10 minutes | Cooking Time: 8 minutes

INGREDIENTS:

- 400g raw prawns, peeled and deveined
- 3 tbsp olive oil
- 4 cloves of garlic, finely chopped
- 50g grated Parmesan cheese
- 1 tsp smoked paprika
- 1 tsp dried oregano
- 1 tsp salt
- 1 tsp black pepper
- 1 lemon, cut into wedges
- fresh parsley, chopped, for garnish

NUTRITION FACTS PER 100G:
Energy: 170 kcal | Protein: 18g | Total Fat: 10g | Saturated Fat: 2g |
Carbohydrates: 2g | Sugars: 0.5g | Dietary Fibre: 1g |

PREPARATION:

1. Begin by preheating the air fryer to 180°C for about 5 minutes.
2. Meanwhile, in a large mixing bowl, combine the olive oil, garlic, smoked paprika, dried oregano, salt, and black pepper.
3. Add the prawns to the bowl and toss them well to ensure they are evenly coated with the seasoning mixture.
4. Once preheated, arrange the seasoned prawns in a single layer in the air fryer basket, avoiding overcrowding. You may need to cook in batches depending on the size of your air fryer.
5. Cook the prawns at 180°C for 4 minutes. Open the air fryer, turn the prawns over, sprinkle the grated Parmesan cheese evenly over them, and cook for an additional 4 minutes or until prawns are cooked through and cheese is slightly crispy.
6. Remove the prawns from the air fryer and transfer to a serving platter.
7. Garnish with fresh parsley and serve immediately with lemon wedges on the side.

SMOKY CHIPOTLE CHICKEN KEBABS

Servings: 4 | Difficulty: Medium | Temperature: 200°C |
Preparation Time: 20 minutes | Cooking Time: 15 minutes

INGREDIENTS:

- 500g chicken breast, cubed
- 2 tbsp olive oil
- 1 tbsp chipotle paste
- 1 tsp smoked paprika
- 1 tsp ground cumin
- 1 tsp garlic powder
- 1 tsp onion powder
- salt, to taste
- black pepper, to taste
- 1 red pepper, chopped into chunks
- 1 yellow pepper, chopped into chunks
- 1 red onion, chopped into chunks
- fresh coriander, chopped (for garnish)
- lemon wedges (for serving)

NUTRITION FACTS PER 100G:
Energy: 112 kcal | Protein: 14g | Total Fat: 5g | Saturated Fat: 0.8g |
Carbohydrates: 3g | Sugars: 1g | Dietary Fibre: 1g

PREPARATION:

1. Begin by placing the chicken breast cubes in a large bowl.
2. In a smaller bowl, mix together olive oil, chipotle paste, smoked paprika, ground cumin, garlic powder, onion powder, salt, and black pepper.
3. Pour this marinade over the chicken, ensuring each piece is thoroughly coated. Let it sit for at least 15 minutes to absorb the flavours.
4. Thread the marinated chicken pieces onto skewers, alternating with red pepper, yellow pepper, and red onion chunks.
5. Preheat the air fryer to 200°C.
6. Arrange the kebabs in the air fryer basket in a single layer.
7. Cook the kebabs for 10-12 minutes, turning halfway through the cooking time, until the chicken is thoroughly cooked and slightly charred on the edges.
8. Garnish with freshly chopped coriander and serve with lemon wedges.

TERIYAKI SALMON BITES

Servings: 4 | Difficulty: Easy | Temperature: 180°C |
Preparation Time: 15 minutes | Cooking Time: 10 minutes

INGREDIENTS:

- 500g salmon fillet, skin removed, cut into bite-sized pieces
- 60ml teriyaki sauce
- 1 tbsp olive oil
- 1 tbsp honey
- 1 clove garlic, minced
- 1 tsp grated ginger
- 1 tbsp sesame seeds
- 2 spring onions, finely chopped
- fresh coriander, chopped, for garnish

NUTRITION FACTS PER 100G:
Energy: 210 kcal | Protein: 16g | Total Fat: 12g | Saturated Fat: 2g |
Carbohydrates: 10g | Sugars: 7g | Dietary Fibre: 0.5g |

PREPARATION:

1. Start by marinating the salmon pieces in a mixture of teriyaki sauce, olive oil, honey, minced garlic, and grated ginger. Ensure each piece is well-coated.
2. Allow the salmon to marinate for about 10 minutes while you preheat your air fryer to 180°C.
3. Once marinated, place the salmon bites in the air fryer basket in a single layer, ensuring they do not overlap.
4. Cook the salmon bites for approximately 10 minutes, shaking the basket halfway through to ensure even cooking.
5. When the cooking time is up, remove the salmon bites carefully and transfer them to a serving dish.
6. Sprinkle the salmon bites with sesame seeds and finely chopped spring onions.
7. Finish by garnishing with freshly chopped coriander before serving.

HERB-CRUSTED SEA BASS FILLETS

Servings: 4 | Difficulty: Medium | Temperature: 180°C |
Preparation Time: 15 minutes | Cooking Time: 12 minutes

INGREDIENTS:

- 4 sea bass fillets (about 150g each)
- 2 tbsp olive oil
- 50g breadcrumbs
- 2 tbsp finely chopped fresh parsley
- 1 tbsp finely chopped fresh thyme
- 1 tbsp finely chopped fresh rosemary
- 1 garlic clove, minced
- salt, to taste
- black pepper, to taste
- lemon wedges, for serving

NUTRITION FACTS PER 100G:
Energy: 170 kcal | Protein: 18g | Total Fat: 10g | Saturated Fat: 2g |
Carbohydrates: 5g | Sugars: 0.5g | Dietary Fibre: 1g |

PREPARATION:

1. Begin by preheating your air fryer to 180°C.
2. Drizzle the sea bass fillets with olive oil, ensuring they are evenly coated.
3. Combine breadcrumbs, parsley, thyme, rosemary, and minced garlic in a shallow dish.
4. Season the breadcrumb mixture with salt and black pepper to taste.
5. Press each sea bass fillet into the breadcrumb mixture, ensuring an even, herb-crusted layer on each side.
6. Place the fillets in the preheated air fryer basket in a single layer.
7. Cook for 12 minutes or until the fillets are golden brown and cooked through.
8. Remove the fillets from the air fryer and serve immediately with lemon wedges.

CHICKEN SKEWERS WITH HERB MARINADE

Servings: 4 | Difficulty: Medium | Temperature: 180°C |
Preparation Time: 30 minutes (plus 1 hour marinating time) | Cooking Time: 15 minutes

INGREDIENTS:

- 500g chicken breast, cut into bite-sized pieces
- 2 tbsp olive oil
- 2 tbsp lemon juice
- 3 cloves garlic, minced
- 1 tsp dried oregano
- 1 tsp dried thyme
- 1 tsp dried rosemary
- 1 tsp paprika
- salt and pepper, to taste
- fresh parsley, chopped (for garnish)

NUTRITION FACTS PER 100G:
Energy: 145 kcal | Protein: 20g | Total Fat: 7g | Saturated Fat: 1g |
Carbohydrates: 2g | Sugars: 0.5g | Dietary Fibre: 1g |

PREPARATION:

1. Begin by preparing the herb marinade. In a large mixing bowl, combine the olive oil, lemon juice, minced garlic, oregano, thyme, rosemary, and paprika. Season with salt and pepper.
2. Add the chicken pieces to the bowl, ensuring they are well-coated with the herb marinade. Cover the bowl with cling film and let it marinate in the refrigerator for at least 1 hour.
3. After marinating, thread the chicken pieces onto skewers, leaving a little space between each piece to ensure even cooking.
4. Preheat your air fryer to 180°C for about 3 minutes.
5. Place the chicken skewers in the air fryer basket, making sure they are not overcrowded. You might need to cook them in batches depending on the size of your air fryer.
6. Cook the chicken skewers for 12-15 minutes, turning them halfway through, until they are golden brown and cooked through.
7. Once cooked, allow the skewers to rest for a couple of minutes, then garnish with fresh chopped parsley before serving.

LEMON GARLIC CALAMARI

Servings: 4 | Difficulty: Easy | Temperature: 180°C |
Preparation Time: 15 minutes | Cooking Time: 10 minutes

INGREDIENTS:

- 400g fresh calamari rings
- 2 tbsp olive oil
- 3 cloves garlic, minced
- juice of 1 lemon
- zest of 1 lemon
- 1 tsp sea salt
- 1/2 tsp black pepper
- 1/2 tsp paprika
- 2 tbsp chopped fresh parsley

NUTRITION FACTS PER 100G:
Energy: 123 kcal | Protein: 15.5g | Total Fat: 6g | Saturated Fat: 1g |
Carbohydrates: 2.5g | Sugars: 1g | Dietary Fibre: 0.6g |

PREPARATION:

1. Begin by preheating your air fryer to 180°C.
2. In a large mixing bowl, combine the olive oil, minced garlic, lemon juice, and lemon zest.
3. Add the calamari rings to the bowl and mix well until the rings are well-coated with the marinade.
4. Sprinkle sea salt, black pepper, and paprika over the calamari, ensuring even seasoning.
5. Allow the calamari to marinate for about 10 minutes to absorb the flavours.
6. Transfer the calamari rings into the air fryer basket, spreading them out in a single layer.
7. Cook the calamari for 10 minutes, or until golden and crispy, shaking the basket halfway through.
8. Once cooked, remove the calamari from the air fryer and set it on a serving plate.
9. Garnish with freshly chopped parsley before serving.

MEDITERRANEAN-SPICED CHICKEN BREASTS

Servings: 4 | Difficulty: Easy | Temperature: 190°C |
Preparation Time: 10 minutes | Cooking Time: 20 minutes

INGREDIENTS:

- 4 chicken breasts (about 150g each)
- 2 tbsp olive oil
- 3 cloves garlic, minced
- 1 tsp paprika
- 1 tsp ground cumin
- 1 tsp ground coriander
- 1 tsp dried oregano
- 1 tsp dried thyme
- 1/2 tsp sea salt
- 1/2 tsp black pepper
- 1 lemon, sliced
- 100g cherry tomatoes, halved

NUTRITION FACTS PER 100G:
Energy: 140 kcal | Protein: 20g | Total Fat: 6g | Saturated Fat: 1g |
Carbohydrates: 2g | Sugars: 1g | Dietary Fibre: 1g |

PREPARATION:

1. Begin by preheating your air fryer to 190°C.
2. In a small bowl, combine the olive oil, minced garlic, paprika, ground cumin, ground coriander, dried oregano, dried thyme, sea salt, and black pepper.
3. Rub this spice mix generously over the chicken breasts, ensuring they are well coated.
4. Place the chicken breasts in the air fryer basket in a single layer, making sure they do not touch each other.
5. Add the lemon slices and halved cherry tomatoes around the chicken for extra flavour.
6. Air fry the chicken breasts for 20 minutes, flipping them halfway through to ensure even cooking.
7. Once cooked, remove from the air fryer and let them rest for a few minutes before serving.

HONEY MUSTARD GLAZED SALMON

Servings: 4 | Difficulty: Easy | Temperature: 180°C |
Preparation Time: 10 minutes | Cooking Time: 12 minutes

INGREDIENTS:

- 4 salmon fillets (approximately 150g each)
- 3 tbsp honey
- 2 tbsp wholegrain mustard
- 1 tbsp Dijon mustard
- 1 tbsp olive oil
- 1 tbsp lemon juice
- salt, to taste
- black pepper, to taste
- fresh coriander for garnish (optional)

NUTRITION FACTS PER 100G:
Energy: 177 kcal | Protein: 17g | Total Fat: 9g | Saturated Fat: 1.5g |
Carbohydrates: 7g | Sugars: 6g | Dietary Fibre: 0g |

PREPARATION:

1. Begin by preheating the air fryer to 180°C.
2. In a small bowl, whisk together the honey, wholegrain mustard, Dijon mustard, olive oil, and lemon juice.
3. Season the salmon fillets with salt and black pepper on both sides.
4. Brush the honey mustard mixture generously over each salmon fillet, ensuring they are well coated.
5. Carefully place the salmon fillets in the air fryer basket, making sure they are not overlapping.
6. Cook the salmon in the preheated air fryer for 12 minutes, or until the fish flakes easily with a fork.
7. Once done, remove the salmon from the air fryer and garnish with fresh coriander if desired.
8. Serve immediately and enjoy your delicious honey mustard glazed salmon!

CAJUN-SPICED CHICKEN PIECES

Servings: 4 | Difficulty: Medium | Temperature: 200°C |
Preparation Time: 15 minutes | Cooking Time: 20 minutes

INGREDIENTS:

- 600g chicken breast pieces
- 3 tbsp olive oil
- 2 tbsp Cajun seasoning
- 1 tsp smoked paprika
- 1 tsp garlic powder
- 1 tsp onion powder
- 1/2 tsp salt
- 1/2 tsp black pepper
- 1 tbsp lemon juice
- fresh parsley, chopped for garnish (optional)

NUTRITION FACTS PER 100G:
Energy: 155 kcal | Protein: 21g | Total Fat: 7g | Saturated Fat: 1g |
Carbohydrates: 1g | Sugars: 0g | Dietary Fibre: 0.5g |

PREPARATION:

1. Combine olive oil, Cajun seasoning, smoked paprika, garlic powder, onion powder, salt, black pepper, and lemon juice in a large bowl.
2. Mix thoroughly to form a marinade.
3. Incorporate the chicken pieces into the bowl, ensuring they are uniformly coated with the marinade.
4. Allow the chicken to marinate for at least 10 minutes.
5. Preheat the air fryer to 200°C.
6. Place the marinated chicken pieces in the air fryer basket, without overcrowding.
7. Cook the chicken for 20 minutes, turning halfway through to ensure even cooking.
8. Check that the chicken pieces are golden brown and fully cooked before removing them from the air fryer.
9. Transfer the cooked chicken pieces to a serving plate and garnish with chopped fresh parsley if desired.

PRAWNS STUFFED WITH HERB CREAM CHEESE

Servings: 4 | Difficulty: Easy | Temperature: 180°C |
Preparation Time: 15 minutes | Cooking Time: 10 minutes

INGREDIENTS:

- 16 large prawns, shelled and deveined
- 150g cream cheese
- 2 tbsp chopped fresh parsley
- 2 tbsp chopped fresh chives
- 1 garlic clove, minced
- 1 lemon, zested
- salt and pepper to taste
- 1 tbsp olive oil
- lemon wedges, for serving

NUTRITION FACTS PER 100G:
Energy: 164 kcal | Protein: 16g | Total Fat: 11g | Saturated Fat: 7g |
Carbohydrates: 2g | Sugars: 1g | Dietary Fibre: 0.5g |

PREPARATION:

1. Begin by preheating your air fryer to 180°C.
2. In a bowl, mix the cream cheese, fresh parsley, chives, minced garlic, and lemon zest until well combined.
3. Season the herb cream cheese mixture with salt and pepper to taste.
4. Using a small sharp knife, carefully cut a slit down the back of each prawn, making sure not to cut all the way through.
5. Spoon a generous amount of the herb cream cheese mixture into the slit of each prawn, pressing gently to close.
6. Lightly brush each stuffed prawn with olive oil.
7. Place the stuffed prawns in a single layer in the air fryer basket, being careful not to crowd them.
8. Air fry the prawns for 8-10 minutes until they are pink and cooked through, and the cheese is warm and softened.
9. Remove the prawns from the air fryer and serve immediately with lemon wedges on the side.

CRISPY CHICKEN ESCALOPE

Servings: 4 | Difficulty: Medium | Temperature: 180°C |
Preparation Time: 20 minutes | Cooking Time: 15 minutes

INGREDIENTS:

- 500g chicken breast fillets
- 100g plain flour
- 2 large eggs
- 150g panko breadcrumbs
- 50g grated Parmesan cheese
- 1 tsp garlic powder
- 1 tsp paprika
- 1 tsp salt
- 1/2 tsp black pepper
- 3 tbsp olive oil

NUTRITION FACTS PER 100G:
Energy: 247 kcal | Protein: 24g | Total Fat: 9g | Saturated Fat: 2.5g |
Carbohydrates: 18g | Sugars: 1g | Dietary Fibre: 1.5g |

PREPARATION:

1. Start by preheating your air fryer to 180°C.
2. Slice the chicken breast fillets into thin cutlets, ensuring an even thickness.
3. Set up three bowls for coating: one with plain flour, one with beaten eggs, and the last with a mixture of panko breadcrumbs, grated Parmesan cheese, garlic powder, paprika, salt, and black pepper.
4. Coat each chicken cutlet first in the plain flour, ensuring both sides are covered.
5. Next, dip the floured chicken cutlets into the beaten eggs, allowing any excess to drip off.
6. Finally, cover the chicken cutlets thoroughly in the breadcrumb mixture, pressing lightly to adhere.
7. Lightly brush each breaded cutlet with olive oil on both sides.
8. Arrange the chicken cutlets in a single layer in the air fryer basket, ensuring they do not overlap.
9. Cook the chicken escalopes in the air fryer for 12-15 minutes, turning them halfway through for even browning.
10. Once crispy and golden, remove from the air fryer and let rest for a few minutes before serving.

BLACKENED MACKEREL FILLETS

Servings: 2 | Difficulty: Medium | Temperature: 200°C |
Preparation Time: 15 minutes | Cooking Time: 10 minutes

INGREDIENTS:

- 2 mackerel fillets (approximately 300g total)
- 2 tbsp olive oil
- 1 tbsp smoked paprika
- 1 tsp garlic powder
- 1 tsp onion powder
- 1 tsp dried thyme
- 1 tsp dried oregano
- 1 tsp cayenne pepper (adjust to taste)
- 1/2 tsp salt
- 1/2 tsp black pepper
- lemon wedges for serving
- fresh parsley for garnish

NUTRITION FACTS PER 100G:
Energy: 210 kcal | Protein: 16g | Total Fat: 15g | Saturated Fat: 3g |
Carbohydrates: 2g | Sugars: 0.5g | Dietary Fibre: 1g |

PREPARATION:

1. Start by preheating your air fryer to 200°C.
2. In a small bowl, mix together the smoked paprika, garlic powder, onion powder, dried thyme, dried oregano, cayenne pepper, salt, and black pepper.
3. Pat the mackerel fillets dry using kitchen paper to remove any excess moisture.
4. Brush each fillet with olive oil on both sides, ensuring they are well coated.
5. Evenly sprinkle the spice mix over both sides of the mackerel fillets, pressing gently to adhere.
6. Place the fillets in the preheated air fryer basket, skin side down.
7. Air fry the mackerel at 200°C for 10 minutes, or until the fish is cooked through and flakes easily with a fork.
8. Carefully remove the mackerel fillets from the air fryer and transfer to a serving plate.
9. Garnish with fresh parsley and serve immediately with lemon wedges on the side for an added burst of flavour.

CHAPTER 4:
HEARTY MEAT AND GAME DISHES (20 RECIPES)

BEEF WELLINGTON BITES

Servings: 12 | Difficulty: Medium | Temperature: 190°C |
Preparation Time: 30 minutes | Cooking Time: 15 minutes

INGREDIENTS:

- 500g beef fillet, cut into 12 pieces
- 1 tbsp olive oil
- 1 tbsp English mustard
- 200g chestnut mushrooms, finely chopped
- 1 shallot, finely chopped
- 2 cloves garlic, minced
- 50ml double cream
- 1 tbsp chopped fresh thyme
- 1 sheet puff pastry, thawed if frozen
- 1 egg, beaten
- salt and pepper to taste

NUTRITION FACTS PER 100G:
Energy: 250 kcal | Protein: 12g | Total Fat: 18g | Saturated Fat: 7g | Carbohydrates: 14g | Sugars: 1g | Dietary Fibre: 1g |

PREPARATION:

1. Preheat the air fryer to 190°C.
2. Season the beef pieces with salt and pepper. Heat olive oil in a skillet over medium-high heat. Sear the beef pieces for about 1-2 minutes on each side until browned. Remove from heat and brush with English mustard. Cool them completely.
3. In the same skillet, sauté the chopped mushrooms, shallot, and garlic over medium heat until soft and all moisture evaporates, around 5 minutes.
4. Pour in the double cream, stir and cook for another 2 minutes. Mix in chopped thyme and season with salt and pepper. Let the mixture cool.
5. Roll out the puff pastry sheet on a lightly floured surface. Cut it into 12 squares, each large enough to wrap a piece of beef.
6. Place a spoonful of mushroom mixture in the centre of each pastry square. Top with a piece of beef. Fold the pastry over the beef and seal the edges by pressing lightly.
7. Brush each pastry parcel with beaten egg to give it a golden finish.
8. Arrange the wrapped beef bites in the air fryer basket, leaving space between each.
9. Cook at 190°C for 12-15 minutes or until the pastry is golden and crisp.
10. Remove from the air fryer and allow to cool slightly before serving.

CRISPY BREADED PORK ESCALOPES

Servings: 4 | Difficulty: Medium | Temperature: 200°C |
Preparation Time: 15 minutes | Cooking Time: 10 minutes

INGREDIENTS:

- 4 pork escalopes (approximately 150g each)
- 100g plain flour
- 2 large eggs
- 100ml milk
- 150g breadcrumbs
- 2 tbsp olive oil

- 1 tsp salt
- 1 tsp black pepper
- 1 tsp garlic powder
- 1 tsp paprika
- cooking spray

NUTRITION FACTS PER 100G:
Energy: 229 kcal | Protein: 14g | Total Fat: 11g | Saturated Fat: 3g |
Carbohydrates: 19g | Sugars: 1g | Dietary Fibre: 1g |

PREPARATION:

1. Start by preheating your air fryer to 200°C for about 5 minutes.
2. Thump the pork escalopes with a meat tenderiser until they are about 1cm thick.
3. Arrange three separate bowls: one with plain flour, another with beaten eggs combined with milk, and a third with seasoned breadcrumbs. To prepare the breadcrumbs, mix them with salt, black pepper, garlic powder, and paprika.
4. Coat each pork escalope first in flour, shaking off any excess. Then, dip them into the egg mixture, ensuring they are fully coated.
5. Finally, dredge the pork escalopes in the breadcrumb mixture, pressing gently to help the crumbs adhere firmly.
6. Lightly sprinkle each breaded escalope with cooking spray to aid in achieving a golden, crispy finish. Also, lightly drizzle with olive oil for extra crispiness.
7. Place the breaded pork escalopes into the air fryer basket, ensuring they are in a single layer and not overlapping. You might need to cook in batches.
8. Cook the pork escalopes in the air fryer for about 10 minutes, flipping halfway through the cooking time to ensure both sides become evenly crispy and golden brown.
9. Once cooked, remove the escalopes from the air fryer and allow them to rest for a minute or two before serving. Serve hot.

HERBED LAMB CUTLETS WITH MINT SAUCE

Servings: 4 | Difficulty: Medium | Temperature: 180°C |
Preparation Time: 20 minutes | Cooking Time: 15 minutes

INGREDIENTS:

- 8 lamb cutlets (approximately 600g)
- 2 tbsp olive oil
- 2 cloves garlic, minced
- 1 tbsp fresh rosemary, chopped
- 1 tbsp fresh thyme, chopped
- salt and black pepper, to taste
- 100ml Greek yoghurt
- 2 tbsp fresh mint, chopped
- 1 tbsp lemon juice
- 1 tsp honey

NUTRITION FACTS PER 100G:
Energy: 207 kcal | Protein: 15g | Total Fat: 15g | Saturated Fat: 6g |
Carbohydrates: 2g | Sugars: 1g | Dietary Fibre: 0.5 g |

PREPARATION:

1. Begin by preheating your air fryer to 180°C.
2. In a small bowl, mix together the olive oil, minced garlic, chopped rosemary, and chopped thyme.
3. Season the lamb cutlets with salt and black pepper.
4. Brush the herbed olive oil mixture generously over both sides of the lamb cutlets.
5. Place the lamb cutlets in the preheated air fryer basket, ensuring they are not overlapping.
6. Cook the lamb cutlets for 12-15 minutes, turning them halfway through the cooking time, until they reach your desired degree of doneness.
7. While the lamb is cooking, prepare the mint sauce by combining the Greek yoghurt, chopped mint, lemon juice, and honey in a bowl. Mix well.
8. Once the lamb cutlets are cooked, remove them from the air fryer and let them rest for a few minutes.
9. Serve the herbed lamb cutlets hot, accompanied by the refreshing mint sauce.

STICKY APPLE-GLAZED PORK RIBS

Servings: 4 | Difficulty: Medium | Temperature: 180°C |
Preparation Time: 15 minutes | Cooking Time: 25 minutes

INGREDIENTS:

- 800g pork ribs
- 2 tbsp olive oil
- 3 cloves garlic, minced
- 100ml apple juice
- 50ml soy sauce
- 2 tbsp apple cider vinegar
- 2 tbsp honey
- 1 tbsp Dijon mustard
- 1 tsp paprika
- 1 tsp ground ginger
- salt and pepper to taste
- fresh parsley, chopped (for garnish)

NUTRITION FACTS PER 100G:
Energy: 238 kcal | Protein: 15g | Total Fat: 17g | Saturated Fat: 5g |
Carbohydrates: 8g | Sugars: 5g | Dietary Fibre: 0.5g |

PREPARATION:

1. Begin by patting the pork ribs dry with a paper towel. Season generously with salt and pepper.
2. In a mixing bowl, whisk together the olive oil, minced garlic, apple juice, soy sauce, apple cider vinegar, honey, Dijon mustard, paprika, and ground ginger.
3. Place the seasoned pork ribs into the air fryer basket, ensuring they are spaced evenly.
4. Set the air fryer to 180°C and preheat for 3 minutes.
5. Brush the ribs generously with the prepared glaze, ensuring they are well-coated.
6. Cook the ribs in the air fryer for 25 minutes, turning and basting with additional glaze halfway through the cooking time.
7. Once cooked through and sticky, remove the ribs from the air fryer and allow them to rest for 5 minutes.
8. Garnish with freshly chopped parsley before serving.

CUMBERLAND SAUSAGE AND MASH BITES

Servings: 4 | Difficulty: Easy | Temperature: 180°C |
Preparation Time: 15 minutes | Cooking Time: 20 minutes

INGREDIENTS:

- 400g Cumberland sausages
- 300g potatoes, peeled and diced
- 30g butter
- 50ml milk
- 50g grated cheddar cheese
- 1 egg, beaten
- 100g breadcrumbs
- 1 tbsp olive oil
- salt and pepper to taste
- fresh parsley, chopped (optional, for garnishing)

NUTRITION FACTS PER 100G:
Energy: 240 kcal | Protein: 8.5g | Total Fat: 16g | Saturated Fat: 6g |
Carbohydrates: 15g | Sugars: 1.5g | Dietary Fibre: 2g |

PREPARATION:

1. Begin by preheating the air fryer to 180°C.
2. Place the diced potatoes in a pot, cover with water, and bring to the boil. Cook until tender, about 10 minutes.
3. Drain the potatoes and mash them with butter, milk, cheddar cheese, salt, and pepper. Set the mash aside to cool.
4. Remove the sausage meat from its casings and mix it thoroughly with the mashed potatoes.
5. Shape the sausage and mash mixture into small, bite-sized balls.
6. Dip each ball into the beaten egg, then coat with breadcrumbs.
7. Lightly brush the balls with olive oil.
8. Arrange the bites in the air fryer basket in a single layer, ensuring they are not touching.
9. Air fry for 10 minutes, then shake the basket to turn the bites and cook for an additional 10 minutes, or until golden and crispy.
10. Garnish with fresh parsley if desired and serve immediately.

LANCASHIRE HOTPOT BITES

Servings: 4 | Difficulty: Medium | Temperature: 180°C |
Preparation Time: 20 minutes | Cooking Time: 25 minutes

INGREDIENTS:

- 400g lamb shoulder, diced
- 1 large onion, finely chopped
- 200g potatoes, thinly sliced
- 1 carrot, finely sliced
- 200ml lamb stock
- 1 tbsp plain flour
- 1 tsp Worcestershire sauce
- 1 tsp dried thyme
- salt and pepper to taste
- 2 tbsp sunflower oil

NUTRITION FACTS PER 100G:
Energy: 145 kcal | Protein: 10g | Total Fat: 8g | Saturated Fat: 3g |
Carbohydrates: 9g | Sugars: 2g | Dietary Fibre: 1g |

PREPARATION:

1. Preheat your air fryer to 180°C.
2. In a large bowl, combine the diced lamb shoulder with plain flour, ensuring each piece is evenly coated.
3. Heat 1 tbsp of sunflower oil in a frying pan over medium heat. Brown the lamb pieces for around 5 minutes, then set aside.
4. Using the same pan, add the remaining oil and sauté the finely chopped onion until softened, about 4 minutes.
5. Return the browned lamb to the pan and add the sliced carrot, lamb stock, Worcestershire sauce, dried thyme, salt, and pepper. Stir well to combine.
6. Transfer the mixture into the air fryer basket and arrange the thinly sliced potatoes on top in an overlapping pattern.
7. Air fry for 20 minutes until the potatoes are golden and crispy, and the lamb is tender.
8. Let the Lancashire Hotpot Bites cool for a couple of minutes before serving.

BRAISED LAMB SHANKS IN RED WINE

Servings: 4 | Difficulty: Medium | Temperature: 180°C |
Preparation Time: 20 minutes | Cooking Time: 2 hours

INGREDIENTS:

- 4 lamb shanks (about 1.2kg)
- 2 tbsp olive oil
- 1 large onion, finely chopped (150g)
- 3 cloves garlic, minced
- 2 carrots, chopped (150g)
- 2 celery stalks, chopped (100g)
- 2 tbsp tomato puree
- 500ml red wine
- 500ml beef stock
- 2 sprigs fresh rosemary
- 2 sprigs fresh thyme
- 2 bay leaves
- salt and pepper, to taste

NUTRITION FACTS PER 100G:
Energy: 125 kcal | Protein: 8g | Total Fat: 8g | Saturated Fat: 3g |
Carbohydrates: 4g | Sugars: 2g | Dietary Fibre: 1g |

PREPARATION:

1. Preheat your air fryer to 180°C.
2. Pat the lamb shanks dry with kitchen paper and season them generously with salt and pepper.
3. Heat 1 tablespoon of olive oil in a large frying pan. Sear the lamb shanks on all sides until browned, about 10 minutes. Set aside.
4. In the same pan, add the remaining olive oil and sauté the onion for 5 minutes until translucent.
5. Toss in the garlic, carrots, and celery, and cook for an additional 5 minutes.
6. Stir in the tomato puree and cook for 2 minutes, letting it coat the vegetables.
7. Pour in the red wine, scraping up any browned bits from the bottom of the pan. Allow the wine to reduce by half, about 10 minutes.
8. Add the beef stock, rosemary, thyme, and bay leaves to the pan and bring to a gentle simmer.
9. Transfer the lamb shanks to your air fryer basket. Pour the wine and vegetable mixture over the lamb shanks.
10. Close the air fryer and set the timer for 2 hours, occasionally checking to ensure the liquid has not evaporated too much. Add more stock if necessary.
11. Once the lamb shanks are tender and falling off the bone, carefully remove them from the air fryer. Discard the bay leaves and herb sprigs.
12. Serve the braised lamb shanks hot with the rich vegetable and red wine sauce spooned over the top.

GARLIC AND ROSEMARY ROAST BEEF

Servings: 4 | Difficulty: Moderate | Temperature: 180°C |
Preparation Time: 15 minutes | Cooking Time: 40 minutes

INGREDIENTS:

- 1kg beef roasting joint
- 4 cloves garlic, minced
- 2 tbsp fresh rosemary, chopped
- 2 tbsp olive oil
- 1 tsp salt
- 1/2 tsp black pepper
- 100ml beef stock

NUTRITION FACTS PER 100G:
Energy: 224 kcal | Protein: 26g | Total Fat: 13g | Saturated Fat: 4.5g |
Carbohydrates: 1g | Sugars: 0g | Dietary Fibre: 0.5g |

PREPARATION:

1. Start by combining the minced garlic, chopped rosemary, olive oil, salt, and black pepper in a small bowl. Mix thoroughly to create a fragrant seasoning paste.
2. Ensure the beef joint is patted dry with kitchen paper to promote even roasting. Coat the beef all over with the seasoned paste, pressing it into the meat to maximise flavour absorption.
3. Preheat the air fryer to 180°C for 5 minutes. This step ensures consistent cooking.
4. Place the seasoned beef joint into the air fryer basket, making sure it's positioned evenly. Pour the beef stock into the bottom of the air fryer basket to keep the meat moist.
5. Allow the beef to roast for 40 minutes, turning it halfway through the cooking time to guarantee an even roast.
6. After 40 minutes, use a meat thermometer to check for desired doneness. Aim for 60°C for medium-rare, adjusting the cooking time as necessary.
7. After removing the beef from the air fryer, let it rest for 10 minutes before slicing to retain juices and ensure a tender, succulent roast.
8. Serve the sliced roast beef with your favourite sides and enjoy a delicious, effortlessly cooked meal.

CRISPY PORK BELLY WITH CRACKLING

Servings: 4 | Difficulty: Medium | Temperature: 200°C |
Preparation Time: 15 minutes + 12 hours (marinating) | Cooking Time: 45 minutes

INGREDIENTS:

- 1kg pork belly, skin scored
- 1 tbsp sea salt
- 2 tsp black pepper, freshly ground
- 1 tsp garlic powder
- 1 tsp smoked paprika
- 1 tbsp vegetable oil
- 1 lemon, cut into wedges (optional)

NUTRITION FACTS PER 100G:
Energy: 518 kcal | Protein: 14g | Total Fat: 52g | Saturated Fat: 18g |
Carbohydrates: 0.5g | Sugars: 0g | Dietary Fibre: 0.1g |

PREPARATION:

1. Begin by scoring the skin of the pork belly in a criss-cross pattern.
2. Rub the sea salt into the skin, ensuring it gets into the scored lines.
3. In a small bowl, mix together the black pepper, garlic powder, and smoked paprika.
4. Apply the spice mixture all over the meat side of the pork belly.
5. Drizzle the vegetable oil over the pork skin and rub it in evenly.
6. Allow the pork belly to marinate in the refrigerator for at least 12 hours, uncovered to let the skin dry out.
7. Preheat your air fryer to 200°C.
8. Place the marinated pork belly into the air fryer basket, skin side up.
9. Cook the pork belly for 30 minutes at 200°C.
10. After 30 minutes, reduce the temperature to 180°C and continue cooking for an additional 15 minutes, or until the skin is crispy and golden brown.
11. Carefully remove the pork belly from the air fryer and let it rest for 10 minutes before slicing.
12. Serve the crispy pork belly with lemon wedges on the side, if desired.

VENISON AND MUSHROOM GAME PIE

Servings: 4 | Difficulty: Medium | Temperature: 180°C |
Preparation Time: 30 minutes | Cooking Time: 25 minutes

INGREDIENTS:

- 400g venison, diced
- 200g mushrooms, sliced
- 1 large onion, finely chopped
- 2 cloves garlic, minced
- 2 tbsp olive oil
- 100ml red wine
- 300ml beef stock

- 1 tbsp tomato purée
- 1 tsp fresh thyme leaves
- 1 tsp fresh rosemary, chopped
- 1 sheet puff pastry
- 1 egg, beaten
- salt and pepper to taste

NUTRITION FACTS PER 100G:
Energy: 180 kcal | Protein: 10g | Total Fat: 11g | Saturated Fat: 4g |
Carbohydrates: 10g | Sugars: 2g | Dietary Fibre: 1g |

PREPARATION:

1. Heat olive oil in a pan over medium heat. Sauté the onions and garlic until they become translucent.
2. Incorporate the diced venison into the pan, searing until browned on all sides.
3. Add the mushrooms and continue to cook until they soften and release their moisture.
4. Pour in the red wine and allow it to reduce by half.
5. Stir in the beef stock, tomato purée, thyme, and rosemary. Simmer for 15 minutes, allowing the mixture to thicken slightly.
6. Adjust seasoning with salt and pepper, then remove from heat and let cool.
7. Roll out the puff pastry on a lightly floured surface and cut it slightly larger than your pie dish.
8. Preheat the air fryer to 180°C.
9. Transfer the venison and mushroom mixture to the pie dish, then cover with the puff pastry, trimming any excess.
10. Brush the pastry with the beaten egg to achieve a golden finish.
11. Place the pie in the air fryer basket and cook for 25 minutes, until the pastry is golden and crispy.
12. Allow the pie to cool for a few minutes before serving.

HONEY-GLAZED DUCK BREAST WITH ORANGE

Servings: 2 | Difficulty: Medium | Temperature: 180°C |
Preparation Time: 15 minutes | Cooking Time: 20 minutes

INGREDIENTS:

- 2 large duck breasts (about 400g)
- 3 tbsp honey
- 1 large orange (zested and juiced, about 100ml juice)
- 1 tsp soy sauce
- 1 clove garlic, minced
- 1 tsp fresh ginger, grated
- salt and pepper, to taste

NUTRITION FACTS PER 100G:
Energy: 220 kcal | Protein: 16g | Total Fat: 10g | Saturated Fat: 3g |
Carbohydrates: 12g | Sugars: 11g | Dietary Fibre: 0.5g |

PREPARATION:

1. Preheat the air fryer to 180°C.
2. Season the duck breasts with salt and pepper on both sides.
3. Combine the honey, orange juice, orange zest, soy sauce, minced garlic, and grated ginger in a small bowl to create the glaze.
4. Place the duck breasts in the air fryer basket, skin-side down, and cook for 10 minutes.
5. Brush the honey-orange glaze over the duck breasts generously.
6. Flip the duck breasts and brush the other side with the glaze.
7. Continue to cook for another 10 minutes, ensuring the duck is cooked through and the skin is crispy.
8. Once cooked, remove the duck breasts from the air fryer and let them rest for 5 minutes.
9. Slice the duck breasts thinly and drizzle with any remaining glaze before serving.
10. Garnish with additional orange zest if desired.

BEEF AND HORSERADISH YORKSHIRE PUDDING WRAPS

Servings: 4 | Difficulty: Medium | Temperature: 200°C |
Preparation Time: 20 minutes | Cooking Time: 20 minutes

INGREDIENTS:

- 200g of roast beef, thinly sliced
- 2 tbsp of horseradish sauce
- 100g of plain flour
- 2 large eggs
- 150ml of milk
- 100ml of water
- 1 tbsp of vegetable oil
- salt and pepper to taste
- fresh parsley, chopped, for garnish

NUTRITION FACTS PER 100G:
Energy: 170 kcal | Protein: 7g | Total Fat: 10g | Saturated Fat: 2g |
Carbohydrates: 14g | Sugars: 2g | Dietary Fibre: 0.5g |

PREPARATION:

1. Begin by preparing the Yorkshire pudding batter. In a mixing bowl, combine the flour and a pinch of salt.
2. Crack the eggs into the bowl and whisk until smooth.
3. Gradually add the milk and water, continuing to whisk until the batter is well combined and smooth.
4. Allow the batter to rest for 10 minutes.
5. Preheat your air fryer to 200°C for 5 minutes.
6. Meanwhile, pour a small amount of vegetable oil into 4 silicon muffin cases (approximately 1/4 tsp in each).
7. Place the muffin cases in the air fryer basket and heat for 3 minutes until the oil is very hot.
8. Carefully remove the basket and evenly distribute the batter into the hot oil-filled muffin cases.
9. Cook in the preheated air fryer for 15 minutes, or until the Yorkshire puddings are crispy and golden brown.
10. While the Yorkshire puddings are cooking, prepare the filling by mixing the horseradish sauce with the roast beef slices.
11. Once the Yorkshire puddings are ready, remove them from the air fryer and let cool for a minute.
12. Gently press down the centre of each pudding to create a well for the filling.
13. Fill each Yorkshire pudding with the horseradish-coated roast beef slices.
14. Season with salt and pepper to taste.
15. Garnish with freshly chopped parsley before serving.

HERB-CRUSTED VENISON FILLET

Servings: 4 | Difficulty: Medium | Temperature: 200°C |
Preparation Time: 20 minutes | Cooking Time: 15 minutes

INGREDIENTS:

- 4 venison fillets (approximately 150g each)
- 2 tbsp olive oil
- 2 cloves garlic, minced
- 1 tbsp fresh rosemary, finely chopped
- 1 tbsp fresh thyme, finely chopped
- 1 tsp coarse sea salt
- 1/2 tsp black pepper
- 1 lemon, zested
- 50g breadcrumbs
- 25g grated Parmesan cheese

NUTRITION FACTS PER 100G:
Energy: 213 kcal | Protein: 23g | Total Fat: 10g | Saturated Fat: 3g |
Carbohydrates: 6g | Sugars: 0.6g | Dietary Fibre: 1g |

PREPARATION:

1. Begin by preheating your air fryer to 200°C.
2. In a small bowl, combine the minced garlic, rosemary, thyme, sea salt, black pepper, and lemon zest.
3. Rub the venison fillets with olive oil, then coat them evenly with the herb mixture.
4. In a separate shallow dish, mix together the breadcrumbs and grated Parmesan cheese.
5. Press each fillet into the breadcrumb mixture, ensuring an even coating on all sides.
6. Place the herb-crusted venison fillets in the air fryer basket, making sure they are not touching each other.
7. Cook for 15 minutes, turning halfway through to ensure even cooking, until the crust is golden and the venison is cooked to your preference.
8. Let the fillets rest for a few minutes before serving to allow juices to redistribute.

SLOW-COOKED OX CHEEK STEW

Servings: 4 | Difficulty: Medium | Temperature: 160°C |
Preparation Time: 20 minutes | Cooking Time: 4 hours

INGREDIENTS:

- 800g ox cheeks, trimmed and cut into chunks
- 2 tbsp olive oil
- 1 large onion, finely chopped
- 2 large carrots, cut into chunks
- 2 celery sticks, chopped
- 3 cloves garlic, minced
- 2 tbsp tomato purée
- 400ml beef stock
- 200ml red wine
- 2 bay leaves
- 1 sprig fresh thyme
- salt and pepper, to taste

NUTRITION FACTS PER 100G:
Energy: 150 kcal | Protein: 12g | Total Fat: 9g | Saturated Fat: 3g |
Carbohydrates: 4g | Sugars: 2g | Dietary Fibre: 1g |

PREPARATION:

1. Begin by preheating your air fryer to 160°C.
2. Heat the olive oil in a large frying pan over medium heat. Brown the ox cheeks in batches, ensuring all sides are seared for maximum flavour.
3. Remove the ox cheeks from the pan and set aside. In the same pan, sauté the onion, carrots, and celery until they start to soften.
4. Stir in the garlic and tomato purée, cooking for an additional 2 minutes until the mixture is fragrant.
5. Return the ox cheeks to the pan, mixing well with the vegetables. Pour in the beef stock and red wine, ensuring the meat is submerged.
6. Add the bay leaves and thyme sprig, and season generously with salt and pepper.
7. Carefully transfer the entire mixture to the air fryer basket, ensuring even distribution.
8. Cook in the air fryer at 160°C for 4 hours, stirring halfway through to ensure even cooking.
9. The ox cheeks should be tender and the sauce rich and flavourful. Serve hot with your choice of mashed potatoes or crusty bread.

SWEET AND SPICY PORK CHOPS

Servings: 4 | Difficulty: Medium | Temperature: 190°C |
Preparation Time: 10 minutes | Cooking Time: 15 minutes

INGREDIENTS:

- 4 pork chops (about 150g each)
- 2 tbsp olive oil
- 3 tbsp honey
- 2 tbsp soy sauce
- 1 tbsp sriracha sauce (or any hot sauce)
- 1 tsp garlic powder
- 1 tsp smoked paprika
- 1 tsp ground cumin
- salt and pepper to taste
- fresh coriander, chopped (for garnish)

NUTRITION FACTS PER 100G:
Energy: 210 kcal | Protein: 15g | Total Fat: 12g | Saturated Fat: 3g |
Carbohydrates: 12g | Sugars: 10g | Dietary Fibre: 0.5g |

PREPARATION:

1. Begin by preheating the air fryer to 190°C.
2. Meanwhile, in a small bowl, combine the honey, soy sauce, sriracha sauce, garlic powder, smoked paprika, and ground cumin.
3. Next, season the pork chops with salt and pepper on both sides.
4. Brush both sides of each pork chop with the olive oil to ensure they're nicely coated.
5. Proceed to drizzle the sweet and spicy sauce mixture over the pork chops, ensuring they are well covered.
6. Once the air fryer is preheated, place the pork chops into the basket, making sure they are in a single layer and not overlapping.
7. Cook for 12-15 minutes, flipping the chops halfway through the cooking time to ensure even browning.
8. Finally, remove the pork chops from the air fryer, garnish with freshly chopped coriander, and serve immediately.

STEAK AND ALE PASTIES

Servings: 4 | Difficulty: Medium | Temperature: 200°C |
Preparation Time: 20 minutes | Cooking Time: 25 minutes

INGREDIENTS:

- 200g trimmed minced beef
- 100ml ale
- 1 medium onion, finely chopped
- 1 medium carrot, diced
- 2 cloves garlic, minced
- 1 tbsp tomato purée
- 1 tbsp Worcestershire sauce

- 1 tbsp plain flour
- 1 tsp salt
- 1/2 tsp black pepper
- 1/2 tsp thyme
- 250g ready-made short crust pastry
- 1 egg, beaten
- 2 tbsp olive oil

NUTRITION FACTS PER 100G:
Energy: 236 kcal | Protein: 9g | Total Fat: 15g | Saturated Fat: 5g |
Carbohydrates: 14g | Sugars: 2g | Dietary Fibre: 1g |

PREPARATION:

1. Begin by heating olive oil in a pan over medium heat. Add onion, carrot, and garlic; sauté until softened.
2. Stir in the minced beef and cook until browned.
3. Combine tomato purée, Worcestershire sauce, ale, salt, pepper, and thyme with the beef mixture.
4. Reduce heat and sprinkle flour over the mixture. Stir well until thickened. Allow to simmer for 5 minutes, then remove from heat.
5. Roll out the short crust pastry on a floured surface and cut into 4 equal circles.
6. Spoon the beef mixture onto one half of each pastry circle, then fold over to create a semi-circle. Press edges together to seal and crimp with a fork.
7. Preheat the air fryer to 200°C.
8. Brush the pasties with beaten egg for a golden finish.
9. Arrange pasties in the air fryer basket in a single layer. Cook at 200°C for 20-25 minutes, or until golden brown and crisp.
10. Remove from the air fryer and allow to cool slightly before serving.

CRISPY LAMB AND MINT SAMOSAS

Servings: 12 samosas | Difficulty: Medium | Temperature: 180°C |
Preparation Time: 30 minutes | Cooking Time: 15 minutes

INGREDIENTS:

- 200g minced lamb
- 1 small onion, finely chopped
- 2 garlic cloves, minced
- 1 tsp grated ginger
- 1 green chilli, finely chopped
- 1 tsp ground cumin
- 1 tsp ground coriander
- 1/2 tsp ground turmeric
- 1/2 tsp garam masala
- salt, to taste
- 2 tbsp fresh mint leaves, finely chopped
- 2 tbsp fresh coriander leaves, finely chopped
- 1 tbsp lemon juice
- 1 packet samosa pastry sheets (about 12 sheets)
- 2 tbsp vegetable oil
- 2 tbsp plain flour
- water, as needed

NUTRITION FACTS PER 100G:
Energy: 230 kcal | Protein: 10g | Total Fat: 15g | Saturated Fat: 5g |
Carbohydrates: 15g | Sugars: 2g | Dietary Fibre: 2g |

PREPARATION:

1. Begin by heating a non-stick pan over medium heat and adding the minced lamb. Cook until the lamb is browned, breaking it up with a wooden spoon as it cooks.
2. Stir in the finely chopped onion, minced garlic, and grated ginger into the lamb. Sauté for about 3-4 minutes until the onions soften.
3. Continue by adding the chopped green chilli, ground cumin, ground coriander, ground turmeric, and garam masala. Mix well and season with salt to taste.
4. Reduce the heat and cook the mixture for an additional 5 minutes, allowing the spices to infuse into the lamb. Remove from heat and allow the mixture to cool slightly.
5. Once cooled, stir in the chopped mint leaves, chopped coriander leaves, and lemon juice. This becomes your samosa filling.
6. Cut each samosa pastry sheet into 3 equal rectangles. To seal the samosas, mix the plain flour with a bit of water to form a thick paste.
7. Lay one rectangle of pastry on a clean surface, place a spoonful of lamb mixture at one end, and fold the pastry into a triangular shape, sealing the edges with the flour paste. Repeat with remaining pastries and filling.
8. Preheat your air fryer to 180°C.
9. Brush each samosa with a small amount of vegetable oil to give it a golden, crispy texture.
10. Place the samosas in the air fryer basket in a single layer to ensure even cooking.
11. Cook the samosas in the air fryer for 12-15 minutes, turning them halfway through the cooking time, until they are golden and crispy.
12. Once done, remove from the air fryer and let cool slightly before serving.

BEEF AND STILTON PIES

Servings: 4 | Difficulty: Medium | Temperature: 180°C |
Preparation Time: 25 minutes | Cooking Time: 20 minutes

INGREDIENTS:

- 400g beef mince
- 100g Stilton cheese, crumbled
- 1 onion, finely chopped
- 2 cloves garlic, minced
- 1 tbsp olive oil
- 200ml beef stock
- 2 tbsp Worcestershire sauce
- 1 tbsp tomato purée
- 2 tbsp plain flour
- 1 sheet puff pastry
- 1 egg, beaten
- salt and pepper, to taste

NUTRITION FACTS PER 100G:
Energy: 250 kcal | Protein: 12g | Total Fat: 18g | Saturated Fat: 8g |
Carbohydrates: 15g | Sugars: 2g | Dietary Fibre: 1g |

PREPARATION:

1. Start by heating the olive oil in a frying pan over medium heat. Sauté the onion and garlic until softened.
2. Add the beef mince to the pan and cook until browned. Stir in the flour until fully combined.
3. Gradually pour in the beef stock, Worcestershire sauce, and tomato purée. Allow the mixture to simmer until thickened.
4. Season with salt and pepper, then add the crumbled Stilton cheese, stirring until well incorporated. Remove from heat and set aside to cool slightly.
5. Roll out the puff pastry sheet and cut into 8 even squares.
6. Spoon the beef mixture onto the centre of 4 pastry squares, leaving a small border around the edges.
7. Place the remaining pastry squares on top, pressing the edges together with a fork to seal.
8. Brush the tops with the beaten egg for a golden finish.
9. Preheat your air fryer to 180°C.
10. Place the pies in the air fryer basket, ensuring they do not touch.
11. Cook for 20 minutes or until the pastry is golden brown and crispy.
12. Carefully remove the pies from the air fryer and allow to cool slightly before serving.

ROAST PHEASANT WITH SAGE AND ONION STUFFING

Servings: 4 | Difficulty: Medium | Temperature: 180°C |
Preparation Time: 20 minutes | Cooking Time: 45 minutes

INGREDIENTS:

- 1 whole pheasant (approximately 1-1.2kg)
- 100g breadcrumbs
- 1 medium onion, finely chopped
- 2 tbsp fresh sage, chopped
- 50g butter
- 1 large egg, beaten
- 1 tsp salt
- 1 tsp black pepper
- 1 lemon, halved
- 2 tbsp olive oil

NUTRITION FACTS PER 100G:
Energy: 200 kcal | Protein: 17g | Total Fat: 13g | Saturated Fat: 3g |
Carbohydrates: 5g | Sugars: 1g | Dietary Fibre: 1g |

PREPARATION:

1. Begin by preheating your air fryer to 180°C.
2. In a frying pan, melt the butter and sauté the finely chopped onion until softened.
3. Combine the sautéed onions, breadcrumbs, and fresh sage in a mixing bowl.
4. Mix in the beaten egg and season with 1 tsp of salt and 1 tsp of black pepper.
5. Stuff the cavity of the pheasant with the sage and onion mixture.
6. Secure the stuffing by tying the legs of the pheasant together with kitchen string.
7. Rub the outside of the pheasant with olive oil, ensuring it's evenly coated.
8. Season the exterior with a pinch of salt and black pepper, then squeeze the juice of half a lemon over the bird.
9. Place the stuffed pheasant breast-side down in the air fryer basket.
10. Cook for 25 minutes, then turn the pheasant over and continue to air fry for an additional 20 minutes until golden and cooked through.
11. Check the internal temperature to ensure it reaches 74°C.
12. Once done, let the pheasant rest for 10 minutes before carving.

SPICED LAMB KOFTA WITH MINT YOGHURT DIP

Servings: 4 | Difficulty: Medium | Temperature: 180°C |
Preparation Time: 20 minutes | Cooking Time: 15 minutes

INGREDIENTS:

- 500g minced lamb
- 1 small onion, finely chopped
- 2 cloves garlic, minced
- 1 tsp ground cumin
- 1 tsp ground coriander
- 1 tsp ground cinnamon

- 1 tsp ground paprika
- 1/2 tsp ground allspice
- 1/2 tsp salt
- 1/2 tsp black pepper
- 2 tbsp fresh parsley, finely chopped
- 1 egg

- 100g plain yoghurt
- 1 tbsp fresh mint, finely chopped
- 1 tbsp lemon juice
- 1/2 tsp honey

NUTRITION FACTS PER 100G:
Energy: 177 kcal | Protein: 12g | Total Fat: 13g | Saturated Fat: 5g |
Carbohydrates: 4g | Sugars: 2g | Dietary Fibre: 0.5g |

PREPARATION:

1. Begin by placing the minced lamb in a mixing bowl.
2. Add the finely chopped onion, minced garlic, ground cumin, ground coriander, ground cinnamon, ground paprika, ground allspice, salt, black pepper, and fresh parsley to the lamb.
3. Crack the egg into the bowl and then mix all the ingredients together thoroughly until well combined.
4. Shape the mixture into small oval-shaped koftas, approximately 2 inches long.
5. Preheat your air fryer to 180°C.
6. Arrange the koftas in a single layer in the air fryer basket, making sure not to overcrowd them.
7. Cook the koftas in the air fryer for 12-15 minutes, turning them halfway through the cooking time for even browning.
8. While the koftas are cooking, prepare the mint yoghurt dip by combining the plain yoghurt, fresh mint, lemon juice, and honey in a small bowl. Stir well to incorporate all the flavours.
9. Once the koftas are done, remove them from the air fryer and let them rest for a couple of minutes.
10. Serve the spiced lamb koftas hot, accompanied by the mint yoghurt dip.

CHAPTER 5:
PLANT-BASED PLEASURES (15 RECIPES)

VEGAN CRISPY AUBERGINE BITES WITH TAHINI DIP

Servings: 4 | Difficulty: Easy | Temperature: 180°C |
Preparation Time: 10 minutes | Cooking Time: 15 minutes

INGREDIENTS:

- 1 large aubergine, cut into bite-sized pieces
- 100g panko breadcrumbs
- 50g plain flour
- 1 tsp smoked paprika
- 1 tsp garlic powder
- 1/2 tsp salt
- 1/4 tsp black pepper
- 100ml unsweetened almond milk
- 3 tbsp olive oil
- 3 tbsp tahini
- 2 tbsp lemon juice
- 1 clove garlic, minced
- 2 tbsp water
- 1 tbsp fresh parsley, finely chopped

NUTRITION FACTS PER 100G:
Energy: 210 kcal | Protein: 4g | Total Fat: 12g | Saturated Fat: 2g |
Carbohydrates: 23g | Sugars: 2g | Dietary Fibre: 4g |

PREPARATION:

1. Begin by preheating the air fryer to 180°C.
2. Mix the plain flour, smoked paprika, garlic powder, salt, and black pepper in a shallow bowl.
3. Pour the almond milk into another shallow bowl.
4. Place the panko breadcrumbs in a third shallow bowl.
5. Dip each aubergine piece into the flour mixture, coating well.
6. Then, dip the coated aubergine into the almond milk.
7. Finally, coat the aubergine pieces with panko breadcrumbs, ensuring an even coating.
8. Arrange the aubergine pieces in a single layer in the air fryer basket; cook in batches if necessary.
9. Drizzle or spray the aubergine pieces lightly with olive oil.
10. Cook for 15 minutes, or until golden brown and crispy, turning halfway through.
11. While the aubergine bites are cooking, prepare the tahini dip by combining tahini, lemon juice, minced garlic, and water in a bowl, mixing until smooth.
12. Garnish the tahini dip with finely chopped parsley.
13. Serve the crispy aubergine bites hot with the tahini dip on the side.

ROASTED VEGETARIAN COURGETTE AND RED PEPPER MEDLEY

Servings: 4 | Difficulty: Easy | Temperature: 180°C |
Preparation Time: 10 minutes | Cooking Time: 15 minutes

INGREDIENTS:

- 2 medium courgettes, sliced
- 1 red pepper, cut into strips
- 1 yellow pepper, cut into strips
- 1 red onion, cut into wedges
- 2 tbsp olive oil
- 1 tsp dried oregano
- 1 tsp dried basil
- salt and black pepper, to taste
- 2 tbsp grated Parmesan cheese
- fresh parsley, chopped (for garnish)

NUTRITION FACTS PER 100G:
Energy: 90 kcal | Protein: 2g | Total Fat: 7g | Saturated Fat: 1g |
Carbohydrates: 5g | Sugars: 3g | Dietary Fibre: 2g |

PREPARATION:

1. Start by preheating your air fryer to 180°C.
2. In a large mixing bowl, combine the sliced courgettes, red and yellow peppers, and red onion wedges.
3. Drizzle the olive oil over the vegetables, then sprinkle with dried oregano, dried basil, salt, and black pepper. Toss everything together until the vegetables are well coated.
4. Transfer the vegetable mixture to the air fryer basket, ensuring they are spread out evenly.
5. Cook the vegetables in the air fryer for 15 minutes, shaking the basket halfway through to ensure even cooking.
6. Once the vegetables are tender and slightly charred, remove them from the air fryer and transfer to a serving dish.
7. Sprinkle the roasted vegetables with grated Parmesan cheese and garnish with freshly chopped parsley.
8. Serve immediately and enjoy your delicious roasted vegetarian courgette and red pepper medley.

SPICY VEGAN CHICKPEA AND SWEET POTATO PATTIES

Servings: 4 | Difficulty: Medium | Temperature: 180°C |
Preparation Time: 20 minutes | Cooking Time: 15 minutes

INGREDIENTS:

- 1 large sweet potato (about 300g), peeled and diced
- 1 can (400g) chickpeas, drained and rinsed
- 1 small red onion, finely chopped
- 2 cloves garlic, minced
- 2 tbsp fresh coriander, chopped
- 1 tsp ground cumin
- 1 tsp smoked paprika
- 1/2 tsp ground cayenne pepper (adjust to taste)
- 3 tbsp plain flour
- 2 tbsp olive oil
- salt and black pepper, to taste
- olive oil spray

NUTRITION FACTS PER 100G:
Energy: 150 kcal | Protein: 3.5g | Total Fat: 4.5g | Saturated Fat: 0.6g |
Carbohydrates: 22g | Sugars: 3g | Dietary Fibre: 4g |

PREPARATION:

1. Begin by boiling the sweet potato in a large pot of water for 10 minutes or until tender. Drain and set aside.
2. Meanwhile, in a large bowl, mash the chickpeas until mostly smooth with some chunks remaining.
3. Add the cooked sweet potato to the mashed chickpeas and combine well.
4. Stir in the chopped red onion, minced garlic, fresh coriander, cumin, smoked paprika, cayenne pepper, and plain flour. Mix until everything is well incorporated.
5. Season the mixture with salt and black pepper.
6. Shape the mixture into 8 small patties.
7. Preheat your air fryer to 180°C for 5 minutes.
8. Lightly spray the air fryer basket with olive oil spray.
9. Arrange the patties in a single layer in the basket, ensuring they do not touch each other.
10. Lightly spray the tops of the patties with olive oil.
11. Cook in the air fryer for 15 minutes, flipping halfway through, until golden brown and crispy.
12. Serve immediately with your favourite dip or salad.

HERB-CRUSTED VEGETARIAN CAULIFLOWER STEAKS

Servings: 4 | Difficulty: Easy | Temperature: 190°C |
Preparation Time: 15 minutes | Cooking Time: 25 minutes

INGREDIENTS:

- 1 large cauliflower head
- 3 tbsp olive oil
- 2 tsp dried oregano
- 2 tsp dried thyme
- 2 tsp dried basil
- 1 tsp garlic powder
- 1 tsp onion powder
- salt, to taste
- black pepper, to taste
- 50g grated parmesan cheese (optional)
- fresh parsley, chopped (for garnish)

NUTRITION FACTS PER 100G:
Energy: 110 kcal | Protein: 3g | Total Fat: 9g | Saturated Fat: 2g |
Carbohydrates: 6g | Sugars: 2g | Dietary Fibre: 3g |

PREPARATION:

1. Begin by preheating the air fryer to 190°C.
2. Meanwhile, remove the leaves and trim the stem of the cauliflower. Slice it vertically into 1.5-2cm thick 'steaks'.
3. In a mixing bowl, combine the olive oil, oregano, thyme, basil, garlic powder, onion powder, salt, and black pepper.
4. Brush the cauliflower steaks generously with the herb mixture on both sides.
5. Place the cauliflower steaks in the air fryer basket in a single layer. It's okay if you need to do this in batches.
6. Air fry for 15 minutes, then flip the steaks and continue cooking for an additional 10 minutes, until golden brown and tender.
7. If using, sprinkle the grated parmesan cheese over the steaks in the last 5 minutes of cooking.
8. Remove from the air fryer and garnish with fresh parsley before serving.

VEGAN BUTTERNUT SQUASH AND SAGE FRITTERS

Servings: 4 | Difficulty: Easy | Temperature: 180°C |
Preparation Time: 20 minutes | Cooking Time: 15 minutes

INGREDIENTS:

- 400g butternut squash, peeled and grated
- 100g chickpea flour
- 50ml water
- 1 small red onion, finely chopped
- 2 cloves garlic, minced
- 1 tbsp fresh sage, finely chopped
- 1 tsp ground cumin
- salt and pepper to taste
- 2 tbsp olive oil

NUTRITION FACTS PER 100G:
Energy: 115 kcal | Protein: 4g | Total Fat: 4g | Saturated Fat: 0.6g |
Carbohydrates: 16g | Sugars: 3g | Dietary Fibre: 4g |

PREPARATION:

1. Start by grating the butternut squash into a large mixing bowl.
2. In a separate bowl, mix the chickpea flour and water to create a smooth batter.
3. Combine the grated butternut squash, chopped red onion, minced garlic, and finely chopped sage in the large bowl.
4. Sprinkle the ground cumin, salt, and pepper over the mixture.
5. Pour the chickpea flour batter into the vegetable mix and stir well to combine.
6. Shape the mixture into small fritters, about the size of a golf ball, then flatten slightly.
7. Lightly brush the fritters with olive oil on both sides.
8. Preheat the air fryer to 180°C.
9. Carefully place the fritters in the air fryer basket, making sure they do not overlap.
10. Cook the fritters for 15 minutes, flipping them over halfway through, until they are golden and crispy.
11. Once done, remove the fritters from the air fryer and let them cool slightly before serving.

ROASTED GARLIC AND ROSEMARY POTATOES

Servings: 4 | Difficulty: Easy | Temperature: 200°C |
Preparation Time: 10 minutes | Cooking Time: 20 minutes

INGREDIENTS:

- 500g baby potatoes, halved
- 2 tbsp olive oil
- 4 cloves garlic, minced
- 1 tbsp fresh rosemary, chopped
- 1 tsp sea salt
- 1/2 tsp black pepper

NUTRITION FACTS PER 100G:
Energy: 140 kcal | Protein: 2g | Total Fat: 6g | Saturated Fat: 1g |
Carbohydrates: 20g | Sugars: 1g | Dietary Fibre: 3g |

PREPARATION:

1. Initially, preheat your air fryer to 200°C.
2. Meanwhile, in a large bowl, combine the halved baby potatoes, olive oil, minced garlic, and chopped rosemary.
3. Sprinkle the sea salt and black pepper over the mixture, ensuring everything is evenly distributed.
4. Transfer the seasoned potatoes into the air fryer basket, spreading them out in a single layer.
5. Cook for 20 minutes, shaking the basket halfway through to ensure even roasting.
6. Ultimately, check the potatoes for tenderness and golden-brown colour before serving.

CRISPY VEGAN TOFU WITH GINGER SOY GLAZE

Servings: 4 | Difficulty: Easy | Temperature: 200°C |
Preparation Time: 15 minutes | Cooking Time: 25 minutes

INGREDIENTS:

- 400g firm tofu
- 2 tbsp soy sauce
- 1 tbsp apple cider vinegar
- 1 tbsp maple syrup
- 1 tbsp grated fresh ginger
- 2 cloves garlic, minced
- 1 tbsp cornflour
- 2 tbsp sesame oil
- 1 tbsp sesame seeds
- 2 spring onions, sliced
- 2 tbsp fresh coriander, chopped

NUTRITION FACTS PER 100G:
Energy: 140 kcal | Protein: 8g | Total Fat: 9g | Saturated Fat: 1.5g |
Carbohydrates: 7g | Sugars: 3g | Dietary Fibre: 1g |

PREPARATION:

1. Begin by pressing the tofu to remove excess moisture. Cut the tofu into 2cm cubes.
2. In a bowl, mix soy sauce, apple cider vinegar, maple syrup, grated ginger, and minced garlic.
3. Combine the tofu cubes with the marinade, ensuring each piece is well-coated. Marinate for at least 10 minutes.
4. Preheat your air fryer to 200°C.
5. Sprinkle cornflour over the marinated tofu and gently toss to coat evenly.
6. Lightly brush the air fryer basket with 1 tbsp of sesame oil to prevent sticking. Arrange the tofu cubes in a single layer.
7. Air fry the tofu for 20-25 minutes, shaking the basket halfway through to ensure even cooking.
8. While the tofu cooks, toast the sesame seeds in a dry pan over medium heat until golden brown.
9. Once the tofu is crispy and golden, transfer it to a serving dish.
10. Garnish tofu with toasted sesame seeds, sliced spring onions, and chopped coriander.
11. Drizzle with remaining sesame oil if desired. Serve immediately and enjoy your crispy vegan tofu with ginger soy glaze.

ROASTED VEGETARIAN VEGETABLE AND LENTIL SALAD

Servings: 4 | Difficulty: Easy | Temperature: 180°C |
Preparation Time: 15 minutes | Cooking Time: 20 minutes

INGREDIENTS:

- 200g red lentils, cooked
- 1 red pepper, diced
- 1 yellow pepper, diced
- 1 courgette, sliced
- 1 aubergine, diced
- 1 red onion, sliced
- 2 tbsp olive oil
- 1 tsp smoked paprika
- 1 tsp ground cumin
- 1 tsp garlic powder
- 100g cherry tomatoes, halved
- 50g feta cheese, crumbled
- 1 handful fresh coriander, chopped
- salt and pepper to taste
- juice of 1 lemon

NUTRITION FACTS PER 100G:
Energy: 97 kcal | Protein: 3.5g | Total Fat: 4.5g | Saturated Fat: 1.0g |
Carbohydrates: 9.2g | Sugars: 3.0g | Dietary Fibre: 3.6g |

PREPARATION:

1. Preheat the air fryer to 180°C.
2. In a large bowl, toss the diced peppers, courgette, aubergine, and red onion with olive oil, smoked paprika, ground cumin, and garlic powder until well-coated.
3. Place the vegetable mixture into the air fryer basket in a single layer and cook for 15 minutes, shaking halfway through.
4. Meanwhile, in a serving bowl, combine the cooked red lentils and cherry tomatoes.
5. Once the vegetables are roasted, add them to the lentil mixture.
6. Sprinkle the crumbled feta cheese and chopped coriander over the salad.
7. Season with salt and pepper to taste.
8. Drizzle with lemon juice before serving.

VEGAN COURGETTE AND CORN FRITTERS

Servings: 4 | Difficulty: Easy | Temperature: 180°C |
Preparation Time: 15 minutes | Cooking Time: 15 minutes

INGREDIENTS:

- 300g courgettes, grated
- 150g sweetcorn, drained
- 100g plain flour
- 50ml almond milk
- 1 small red onion, finely chopped
- 2 garlic cloves, minced
- 1 tbsp ground flaxseed
- 3 tbsp water
- 1 tsp baking powder
- 1 tsp paprika
- 1 tsp ground cumin
- salt and pepper to taste
- 2 tbsp olive oil (for brushing)

NUTRITION FACTS PER 100G:
Energy: 138 kcal | Protein: 4g | Total Fat: 5g | Saturated Fat: 0.7g |
Carbohydrates: 18g | Sugars: 2g | Dietary Fibre: 3g |

PREPARATION:

1. Start by mixing the ground flaxseed and water in a small bowl. Allow it to sit for a few minutes until it thickens.
2. In a large mixing bowl, combine the grated courgettes, sweetcorn, and finely chopped red onion. Mix well.
3. Next, stir in the minced garlic, thickened flaxseed mixture, plain flour, almond milk, baking powder, paprika, ground cumin, salt, and pepper.
4. Mix everything thoroughly until you achieve a batter-like consistency.
5. Preheat your air fryer to 180°C.
6. Shape the mixture into small fritters and brush each side lightly with olive oil.
7. Arrange the fritters in the air fryer basket, making sure not to overcrowd them.
8. Cook for 10-15 minutes, flipping halfway through, until they are golden brown and crispy.
9. Serve the fritters hot with your favourite dip or salad.

SMOKY BBQ VEGAN JACKFRUIT SLIDERS

Servings: 4 | Difficulty: Easy | Temperature: 180°C |
Preparation Time: 15 minutes | Cooking Time: 20 minutes

INGREDIENTS:

- 400g young jackfruit (canned, in water or brine)
- 1 small red onion, finely sliced
- 2 garlic cloves, minced
- 100ml smoky BBQ sauce
- 1 tsp smoked paprika

- 1 tbsp olive oil
- 4 slider buns
- 50g pickled red cabbage
- fresh coriander leaves, for garnish
- salt and pepper, to taste

NUTRITION FACTS PER 100G:
Energy: 145 kcal | Protein: 2.5g | Total Fat: 4.5g | Saturated Fat: 0.8g |
Carbohydrates: 23g | Sugars: 6.5g | Dietary Fibre: 3.5 g |

PREPARATION:

1. Begin by preheating your air fryer to 180°C.
2. Drain and rinse the canned jackfruit. Gently squeeze out excess water, then shred using your hands or a fork.
3. In a mixing bowl, toss the shredded jackfruit with the smoked paprika, minced garlic, salt, and pepper.
4. Heat olive oil in a pan over medium heat. Sauté the sliced red onion until soft and translucent, about 3-4 minutes.
5. Add the seasoned jackfruit to the pan and cook for another 5 minutes, stirring occasionally.
6. Pour in the smoky BBQ sauce and mix well. Allow to simmer for 2-3 minutes until heated through.
7. Transfer the BBQ jackfruit mixture to your air fryer basket, spreading it out evenly. Cook for 10-12 minutes, shaking the basket halfway through to ensure even cooking.
8. Lightly toast the slider buns in the air fryer for 3 minutes.
9. Assemble the sliders by adding a generous portion of BBQ jackfruit onto the bottom bun, topping with pickled red cabbage and fresh coriander leaves.
10. Complete with the top bun and serve immediately.

CRISPY VEGAN POLENTA CHIPS WITH CHILLI DIP

Servings: 4 | Difficulty: Easy | Temperature: 200°C |
Preparation Time: 20 minutes | Cooking Time: 25 minutes

INGREDIENTS:

- 250g instant polenta
- 1 litre vegetable broth
- 2 tbsp olive oil
- 1 tsp garlic powder
- 1 tsp paprika
- 1 tsp dried oregano

- salt and pepper to taste
- 1 red chilli, finely chopped
- 2 tbsp vegan mayonnaise
- 1 tbsp sriracha sauce
- juice of half a lime
- fresh coriander, chopped (for garnish)

NUTRITION FACTS PER 100G:
Energy: 109 kcal | Protein: 2.2g | Total Fat: 4.1g | Saturated Fat: 0.7g |
Carbohydrates: 15.2g | Sugars: 0.8g | Dietary Fibre: 2.1g |

PREPARATION:

1. Bring the vegetable broth to a boil in a large saucepan. Gradually whisk in the polenta.
2. Reduce the heat to low and cook the polenta, stirring frequently, until thickened, about 5 minutes.
3. Spread the cooked polenta onto a baking tray lined with parchment paper, smoothing it out to a thickness of about 1cm. Allow it to cool and firm up, roughly 15 minutes.
4. Once set, cut the polenta into chip-sized pieces.
5. Preheat your air fryer to 200°C.
6. In a large bowl, toss the polenta chips with olive oil, garlic powder, paprika, oregano, salt, and pepper until evenly coated.
7. Arrange the polenta chips in a single layer in the air fryer basket. You might need to do this in batches.
8. Cook for 15-20 minutes, shaking the basket halfway through, until the chips are golden and crispy.
9. While the chips are cooking, prepare the chilli dip. In a small bowl, mix the vegan mayonnaise, sriracha sauce, lime juice, and chopped red chilli.
10. Transfer the crispy polenta chips to a plate, garnish with fresh coriander, and serve immediately with the chilli dip.

ROASTED VEGAN BRUSSELS SPROUTS WITH BALSAMIC GLAZE

Servings: 4 | Difficulty: Easy | Temperature: 180°C |
Preparation Time: 10 minutes | Cooking Time: 15 minutes

INGREDIENTS:

- 500g Brussels sprouts, halved
- 2 tbsp olive oil
- 1/2 tsp sea salt
- 1/4 tsp black pepper
- 2 tbsp balsamic vinegar
- 1 tbsp maple syrup
- 1 tsp Dijon mustard
- 1 clove garlic, minced

NUTRITION FACTS PER 100G:
Energy: 115 kcal | Protein: 2.5g | Total Fat: 5g | Saturated Fat: 0.7g |
Carbohydrates: 14g | Sugars: 5g | Dietary Fibre: 4g |

PREPARATION:

1. Preheat the air fryer to 180°C.
2. In a large bowl, toss Brussels sprouts with olive oil, sea salt, and black pepper until evenly coated.
3. Transfer the Brussels sprouts to the air fryer basket in a single layer.
4. Air fry for 15 minutes, shaking the basket halfway through to ensure even cooking.
5. Meanwhile, whisk together balsamic vinegar, maple syrup, Dijon mustard, and minced garlic in a small bowl to make the glaze.
6. Once the Brussels sprouts are crispy and golden, remove them from the air fryer.
7. Drizzle the balsamic glaze over the roasted Brussels sprouts and toss gently to coat.
8. Serve immediately and enjoy your flavourful, perfectly roasted vegan Brussels sprouts.

STUFFED VEGETARIAN PORTOBELLO MUSHROOMS WITH SPINACH

Servings: 4 | Difficulty: Medium | Temperature: 180°C |
Preparation Time: 15 minutes | Cooking Time: 10 minutes

INGREDIENTS:

- 4 large portobello mushrooms (cleaned and stems removed)
- 200g fresh spinach
- 100g ricotta cheese
- 50g grated parmesan cheese
- 1 small onion (finely chopped)
- 2 garlic cloves (minced)
- 2 tbsp olive oil
- 1 tsp dried basil
- 1 tsp dried oregano
- salt (to taste)
- black pepper (to taste)

NUTRITION FACTS PER 100G:
Energy: 110 kcal | Protein: 5g | Total Fat: 7g | Saturated Fat: 2.5g |
Carbohydrates: 6g | Sugars: 2g | Dietary Fibre: 2g |

PREPARATION:

1. Start by preheating your air fryer to 180°C.
2. In a pan, heat 1 tbsp of olive oil and sauté the chopped onion and minced garlic until softened.
3. Add the fresh spinach, cooking until wilted, then transfer the mixture to a bowl and allow to cool slightly.
4. Mix in the ricotta cheese, grated parmesan, dried basil, dried oregano, salt, and black pepper to the spinach mixture.
5. Brush the portobello mushrooms with the remaining 1 tbsp of olive oil and season with a pinch of salt and pepper.
6. Proceed to stuff each mushroom generously with the spinach and cheese mixture.
7. Carefully place the stuffed mushrooms into the air fryer basket.
8. Air fry for approximately 10 minutes, or until the mushrooms are tender and the filling is golden.
9. Serve immediately, garnished with a sprinkle of fresh basil if desired.

VEGAN FALAFEL WRAPS WITH MINT YOGHURT

Servings: 4 | Difficulty: Medium | Temperature: 180°C |
Preparation Time: 15 minutes | Cooking Time: 20 minutes

INGREDIENTS:

- 400g canned chickpeas, drained and rinsed
- 1 small onion, finely chopped
- 2 cloves garlic, minced
- 30g fresh coriander, chopped
- 30g fresh parsley, chopped
- 1 tsp ground cumin
- 1 tsp ground coriander
- 1/2 tsp ground paprika
- 1/2 tsp baking powder
- 3 tbsp plain flour
- salt and pepper, to taste
- 2 tbsp olive oil
- 4 large tortilla wraps
- 100g mixed salad leaves

Mint Yoghurt:

- 150ml vegan yoghurt
- 1 tbsp fresh mint, finely chopped
- 1/2 lemon, juiced
- salt and pepper, to taste

NUTRITION FACTS PER 100G:
Energy: 180 kcal | Protein: 5.3g | Total Fat: 6.8g | Saturated Fat: 1.0g |
Carbohydrates: 24.9g | Sugars: 2.3g | Dietary Fibre: 4.7g |

PREPARATION:

1. Begin by placing the chickpeas in a food processor along with the chopped onion, garlic, fresh coriander, and parsley. Blitz until you have a coarse mixture.
2. Next, add the ground cumin, ground coriander, paprika, baking powder, and plain flour to the chickpea mixture. Season with salt and pepper, then blend again until everything is well combined.
3. Shape the mixture into small balls or patties, ensuring they are even in size. Gently flatten them.
4. Preheat your air fryer to 180°C for about 5 minutes.
5. Brush the falafel balls with olive oil, then place them in the air fryer basket. Ensure they are in a single layer and not overcrowded.
6. Cook in the air fryer at 180°C for 15-20 minutes, turning halfway through, until they are golden and crispy.
7. While the falafel is cooking, prepare the mint yoghurt by combining the vegan yoghurt, fresh mint, lemon juice, salt, and pepper in a small bowl. Stir until well mixed.
8. Warm the tortilla wraps in a dry frying pan or microwave for a few seconds until pliable.
9. To assemble, place a few mixed salad leaves on each tortilla wrap, top with the crispy falafel, and drizzle with the mint yoghurt.
10. Wrap tightly and serve immediately.

VEGAN SPICED ONION BHAJIS

Servings: 4 | Difficulty: Easy | Temperature: 180°C |
Preparation Time: 15 minutes | Cooking Time: 15 minutes

INGREDIENTS:

- 200g gram flour
- 2 large onions, thinly sliced
- 3 tbsp fresh coriander, chopped
- 1 tsp ground cumin
- 1 tsp ground coriander
- 1 tsp turmeric powder
- 1 tsp mild chilli powder
- 1 tsp baking powder
- 150ml water
- 2 tbsp lemon juice
- salt to taste
- cooking spray

> **NUTRITION FACTS PER 100G:**
> Energy: 150 kcal | Protein: 6g | Total Fat: 2g | Saturated Fat: 0.5g |
> Carbohydrates: 25g | Sugars: 3g | Dietary Fibre: 5g |

PREPARATION:

1. Begin by preheating your air fryer to 180°C.
2. In a large mixing bowl, combine the gram flour, ground cumin, ground coriander, turmeric powder, mild chilli powder, and baking powder. Mix well.
3. Slowly add water to the dry ingredients, stirring constantly to form a smooth batter.
4. Incorporate the thinly sliced onions and chopped fresh coriander into the batter. Mix until the onions are well coated.
5. Add lemon juice and salt to taste, then mix again to ensure everything is evenly distributed.
6. Lightly grease the air fryer basket with cooking spray.
7. Using a spoon, scoop portions of the mixture and place them in the air fryer basket, ensuring they do not touch each other.
8. Spray the tops of the bhajis lightly with cooking spray.
9. Air fry at 180°C for 15 minutes, or until golden and crispy.
10. Remove the bhajis from the air fryer and allow them to cool slightly before serving.

CHAPTER 6:
DESSERTS AND CELEBRATION BAKES (15 RECIPES)

CINNAMON SUGAR CHURROS

Servings: 4 | Difficulty: Medium | Temperature: 180°C |
Preparation Time: 20 minutes | Cooking Time: 12 minutes

INGREDIENTS:

- 100g plain flour
- 240ml water
- 60g unsalted butter
- 1 tbsp granulated sugar
- 1/4 tsp salt

- 1 large egg
- 1/2 tsp vanilla extract
- 100g granulated sugar (for coating)
- 1 tsp ground cinnamon
- cooking spray

NUTRITION FACTS PER 100G:
Energy: 310 kcal | Protein: 4g | Total Fat: 11g | Saturated Fat: 6g |
Carbohydrates: 46g | Sugars: 26g | Dietary Fibre: 1g |

PREPARATION:

1. Begin by preheating your air fryer to 180°C.
2. In a saucepan, combine water, unsalted butter, 1 tbsp sugar, and salt. Bring to a boil over medium heat.
3. Remove from heat, then add plain flour. Stir vigorously until the mixture forms a smooth ball.
4. Let the mixture cool for 5 minutes. After cooling, add the egg and vanilla extract; mix until fully incorporated.
5. Transfer the dough to a piping bag fitted with a star tip.
6. Line the air fryer basket with parchment paper and lightly spray with cooking spray.
7. Pipe the dough into 4-inch strips directly onto the parchment paper.
8. Air fry the churros for 10-12 minutes, flipping them halfway through, until golden brown and crispy.
9. While the churros are cooking, mix together 100g granulated sugar and ground cinnamon in a shallow dish.
10. Once churros are cooked, immediately roll them in the cinnamon-sugar mixture to coat them thoroughly.
11. Serve warm and enjoy your delicious cinnamon sugar churros!

MINI VICTORIA SPONGE CAKES

Servings: 4 | Difficulty: Easy | Temperature: 160°C |
Preparation Time: 15 minutes | Cooking Time: 15 minutes

INGREDIENTS:

- 100g self-raising flour
- 100g caster sugar
- 100g unsalted butter, softened
- 2 large eggs
- 1 tsp vanilla extract
- 2 tbsp milk
- 100ml double cream
- 2 tbsp icing sugar
- 4 tbsp strawberry jam
- extra icing sugar for dusting

NUTRITION FACTS PER 100G:
Energy: 380 kcal | Protein: 4g | Total Fat: 22g | Saturated Fat: 14g |
Carbohydrates: 42g | Sugars: 29g | Dietary Fibre: 0.5g |

PREPARATION:

1. Start by preheating your air fryer to 160°C.
2. Cream together the unsalted butter and caster sugar in a bowl until light and fluffy.
3. Beat in the eggs one at a time, then stir in the vanilla extract and milk.
4. Gradually fold in the self-raising flour until well combined.
5. Evenly distribute the batter into four greased mini cake tins.
6. Carefully place the tins in the preheated air fryer and bake for 12-15 minutes, or until golden and a skewer comes out clean.
7. While the cakes are baking, whip the double cream with 2 tbsp icing sugar until stiff peaks form.
8. Allow the cakes to cool completely.
9. Once cooled, slice each cake in half horizontally to create two layers.
10. Spread a generous layer of strawberry jam on the bottom half of each cake and top with whipped cream.
11. Sandwich the cakes back together and dust the top with extra icing sugar before serving.

STICKY TOFFEE PUDDING BITES

Servings: 12 bites | Difficulty: Medium | Temperature: 180°C |
Preparation Time: 20 minutes | Cooking Time: 10-12 minutes

INGREDIENTS:

- 150g pitted dates
- 175ml boiling water
- 1 tsp bicarbonate of soda
- 60g unsalted butter, softened
- 175g light muscovado sugar
- 2 large eggs
- 175g self-raising flour
- 1 tsp vanilla extract

NUTRITION FACTS PER 100G:
Energy: 342 kcal | Protein: 4g | Total Fat: 10.5g | Saturated Fat: 6g |
Carbohydrates: 58g | Sugars: 40g | Dietary Fibre: 3g |

PREPARATION:

1. Begin by placing the pitted dates in a bowl and pouring over the boiling water. Sprinkle with bicarbonate of soda and leave to soak for 10 minutes.
2. While the dates are soaking, cream together the butter and light muscovado sugar in a mixing bowl until light and fluffy.
3. Beat in the eggs, one at a time, ensuring each is fully absorbed before adding the next.
4. Next, fold in the self-raising flour, creating a smooth batter.
5. Add the soaked dates, including the soaking liquid, and the vanilla extract to the batter, stirring gently to combine.
6. Preheat your air fryer to 180°C.
7. Spoon the mixture into greased, air fryer-safe silicone moulds or ramekins, filling each about two-thirds full.
8. Place the moulds into the air fryer basket and cook for 10-12 minutes, or until a skewer inserted into the centre comes out clean.
9. Once cooked, allow to cool slightly before removing from moulds.
10. Serve warm with a drizzle of toffee sauce or a dollop of double cream.

AIRY LEMON DRIZZLE CAKE BARS

Servings: 12 bars | Difficulty: Easy | Temperature: 180°C |
Preparation Time: 15 minutes | Cooking Time: 20 minutes

INGREDIENTS:

- 200g self-raising flour
- 200g caster sugar
- 200g unsalted butter, softened
- 4 large eggs
- zest of 2 lemons
- juice of 1 lemon
- 50ml milk
- 1 tsp baking powder
- 200g icing sugar
- juice of 1 lemon for the drizzle

NUTRITION FACTS PER 100G:
Energy: 430 kcal | Protein: 4.5g | Total Fat: 23g | Saturated Fat: 14g |
Carbohydrates: 56g | Sugars: 35g | Dietary Fibre: 0.5g |

PREPARATION:

1. Begin by preheating your air fryer to 180°C.
2. In a mixing bowl, cream together the softened butter and caster sugar until light and fluffy.
3. Gradually beat in the eggs, one at a time, ensuring each one is well incorporated before adding the next.
4. Stir in the lemon zest and juice, followed by gently folding in the self-raising flour and baking powder.
5. Add the milk to the mixture and stir until smooth.
6. Line an air fryer-friendly baking tin with parchment paper and pour in the cake batter, spreading it evenly.
7. Place the tin in the air fryer and cook for 20 minutes, or until a skewer inserted into the centre comes out clean.
8. While the cake is cooling, prepare the lemon drizzle by mixing the icing sugar with the lemon juice until smooth.
9. Once the cake is completely cooled, drizzle the lemon icing over the top and allow it to set.
10. Slice into bars and serve.

FRUIT SCONES WITH CLOTTED CREAM

Servings: 8 | Difficulty: Medium | Temperature: 180°C |
Preparation Time: 20 minutes | Cooking Time: 15 minutes

INGREDIENTS:

- 250g self-raising flour
- 50g unsalted butter, cold and cubed
- 50g caster sugar
- 150ml whole milk
- 100g mixed dried fruit (raisins, sultanas, currants)
- 1 egg, beaten (for glazing)
- clotted cream for serving

NUTRITION FACTS PER 100G:
Energy: 300 kcal | Protein: 5g | Total Fat: 6g | Saturated Fat: 3g |
Carbohydrates: 55g | Sugars: 20g | Dietary Fibre: 2g |

PREPARATION:

1. Begin by preheating your air fryer to 180°C.
2. Combine the self-raising flour and cubed butter in a large bowl. Rub together until the mixture resembles breadcrumbs.
3. Stir in the caster sugar and mixed dried fruit.
4. Gradually add the whole milk, mixing until a soft dough forms.
5. Turn the dough onto a lightly floured surface and knead gently.
6. Roll the dough out to about 2cm thick. Cut into rounds using a 5cm cutter.
7. Lightly brush the tops of the scones with the beaten egg.
8. Arrange the scones in the air fryer basket in a single layer. Cook for 12-15 minutes or until golden brown.
9. Allow the scones to cool slightly on a wire rack before serving.

CRISPY APPLE TURNOVERS

Servings: 4 | Difficulty: Easy | Temperature: 180°C |
Preparation Time: 15 minutes | Cooking Time: 10 minutes

INGREDIENTS:

- 1 sheet of puff pastry (approx. 250g)
- 2 medium apples, peeled and diced (about 300g)
- 50g granulated sugar
- 1 tsp ground cinnamon
- 1 tbsp lemon juice
- 1 tsp cornflour
- 1 egg, beaten
- icing sugar, for dusting

NUTRITION FACTS PER 100G:
Energy: 240 kcal | Protein: 3g | Total Fat: 13g | Saturated Fat: 6g |
Carbohydrates: 29g | Sugars: 13g | Dietary Fibre: 2g |

PREPARATION:

1. Begin by preheating your air fryer to 180°C.
2. In a large bowl, mix together the diced apples, granulated sugar, ground cinnamon, lemon juice, and cornflour until thoroughly combined.
3. Roll out the puff pastry on a lightly floured surface and cut it into 8 equal squares.
4. Place a generous spoonful of the apple mixture onto the centre of each pastry square.
5. Lightly brush the edges of the pastry squares with beaten egg.
6. Fold the pastry over the apple filling to create a triangle, pressing the edges together with a fork to seal.
7. Arrange the turnovers in a single layer in the air fryer basket, ensuring they do not touch.
8. Brush the tops of the turnovers with more beaten egg.
9. Air fry for 10 minutes or until golden brown and crispy.
10. Once cooked, remove from the air fryer and allow to cool slightly. Dust with icing sugar before serving.

WARM CHOCOLATE BROWNIE BITES

Servings: 12 | Difficulty: Easy | Temperature: 180°C |
Preparation Time: 10 minutes | Cooking Time: 15 minutes

INGREDIENTS:

- 100g unsalted butter
- 150g dark chocolate, chopped
- 100g caster sugar
- 50g light brown sugar
- 2 large eggs
- 1 tsp vanilla extract

- 90g plain flour
- 20g cocoa powder
- 1/2 tsp baking powder
- pinch of salt
- 50g chocolate chips (optional)

NUTRITION FACTS PER 100G:
Energy: 438 kcal | Protein: 5g | Total Fat: 26g | Saturated Fat: 15g |
Carbohydrates: 46g | Sugars: 31g | Dietary Fibre: 4g |

PREPARATION:

1. Start by melting the butter and dark chocolate in a microwave-safe bowl in 30-second intervals, stirring in between until smooth.
2. Transfer the melted mixture to a mixing bowl and let it cool slightly.
3. Beat in the caster sugar and light brown sugar until well combined.
4. Next, add the eggs one at a time, ensuring each is fully incorporated before adding the next.
5. Stir in the vanilla extract.
6. In another bowl, sift together the plain flour, cocoa powder, baking powder, and salt.
7. Gently fold the dry ingredients into the wet mixture until just combined.
8. For extra indulgence, toss in the chocolate chips and fold them through the batter.
9. Grease a silicone mini muffin mould and evenly distribute the brownie batter into the moulds.
10. Preheat the air fryer to 180°C for 3 minutes.
11. Place the silicone mould in the air fryer basket and cook for 12-15 minutes, or until a toothpick inserted into the centre comes out with a few moist crumbs.
12. Carefully remove the brownie bites from the mould and allow them to cool slightly before serving warm.

CLASSIC BREAD AND BUTTER PUDDING

Servings: 4 | Difficulty: Easy | Temperature: 180°C |
Preparation Time: 15 minutes | Cooking Time: 20 minutes

INGREDIENTS:

- 200g white bread (stale, cut into triangles)
- 50g unsalted butter (softened)
- 350ml whole milk
- 50ml double cream
- 75g caster sugar
- 2 large eggs
- 1 tsp vanilla extract
- 50g sultanas
- 1 tsp ground cinnamon
- 2 tbsp demerara sugar for topping

NUTRITION FACTS PER 100G:
Energy: 231 kcal | Protein: 5g | Total Fat: 10g | Saturated Fat: 6g |
Carbohydrates: 30g | Sugars: 16g | Dietary Fibre: 1g |

PREPARATION:

1. Preheat the air fryer to 180°C.
2. Generously butter each slice of bread on both sides.
3. Arrange half the bread slices in a single layer in a greased air fryer-safe dish. Sprinkle with half the sultanas.
4. Layer the remaining bread slices on top, followed by the rest of the sultanas.
5. In a bowl, whisk together the milk, double cream, caster sugar, eggs, and vanilla extract until smooth.
6. Pour the custard mixture evenly over the bread layers, ensuring all slices are soaked.
7. Let stand for 10 minutes to allow the bread to absorb the custard.
8. Sprinkle the top with ground cinnamon and demerara sugar.
9. Carefully place the dish into the preheated air fryer and cook for 20 minutes until golden brown and set.
10. Remove from the air fryer and let cool for a few minutes before serving.

STICKY GINGER CAKE SLICES

Servings: 12 | Difficulty: Medium | Temperature: 160°C |
Preparation Time: 15 minutes | Cooking Time: 25 minutes

INGREDIENTS:

- 200g self-raising flour
- 1 tsp baking powder
- 2 tsp ground ginger
- 1 tsp ground cinnamon
- 150g unsalted butter, melted
- 200g dark brown sugar
- 2 large eggs
- 100ml whole milk
- 100g golden syrup
- 50g stem ginger, finely chopped

NUTRITION FACTS PER 100G:
Energy: 385 kcal | Protein: 5g | Total Fat: 15g | Saturated Fat: 9g |
Carbohydrates: 57g | Sugars: 39g | Dietary Fibre: 1g |

PREPARATION:

1. Start by preheating the air fryer to 160°C.
2. In a large mixing bowl, sift together the self-raising flour, baking powder, ground ginger, and ground cinnamon.
3. Take another bowl and whisk the melted butter and dark brown sugar until creamy.
4. Beat in the eggs, one at a time, ensuring they are fully incorporated.
5. Stir in the whole milk and golden syrup into the wet mixture.
6. Gradually combine the wet mixture with the dry ingredients, stirring well to avoid lumps.
7. Fold in the finely chopped stem ginger.
8. Grease a suitable baking tin that fits into your air fryer and pour the batter into it.
9. Place the baking tin in the preheated air fryer and cook for 25 minutes or until a skewer inserted into the centre comes out clean.
10. Allow the cake to cool in the tin for 10 minutes before transferring to a wire rack to cool completely.
11. Once cooled, slice the cake into squares or rectangles as desired.

BAKED VANILLA CHEESECAKE BITES

Servings: 12 | Difficulty: Medium | Temperature: 160°C |
Preparation Time: 20 minutes | Cooking Time: 15 minutes

INGREDIENTS:

- 150g digestive biscuits
- 75g unsalted butter, melted
- 300g cream cheese
- 100g granulated sugar
- 2 large eggs
- 1 tsp vanilla extract
- 2 tbsp plain flour
- 100ml double cream

NUTRITION FACTS PER 100G:
Energy: 330 kcal | Protein: 5g | Total Fat: 24g | Saturated Fat: 14g |
Carbohydrates: 24g | Sugars: 15g | Dietary Fibre: 0.5g |

PREPARATION:

1. Start by crushing the digestive biscuits into fine crumbs. Mix with the melted butter until well combined.
2. Press the crumb mixture firmly into the bases of a silicone muffin tray, creating an even layer. Place in the freezer to set.
3. Beat the cream cheese and granulated sugar together until smooth.
4. Add the eggs one at a time, beating well after each addition. Incorporate the vanilla extract.
5. Sift in the plain flour and fold gently into the mixture.
6. Gradually mix in the double cream until fully combined and smooth.
7. Pour the cream cheese mixture over the chilled biscuit bases, filling each mould almost to the top.
8. Preheat the air fryer to 160°C.
9. Place the muffin tray into the air fryer and cook for 15 minutes. Cheesecake bites should be set but slightly soft in the centre.
10. Allow to cool completely in the tray before removing. Chill in the fridge for at least 2 hours before serving.

AIRY MERINGUE NESTS WITH BERRIES

Servings: 4 | Difficulty: Medium | Temperature: 100°C |
Preparation Time: 15 minutes | Cooking Time: 60 minutes

INGREDIENTS:

- 4 large egg whites
- 200g caster sugar
- 1 tsp vanilla extract
- 1 tsp white vinegar
- 300g mixed berries (strawberries, raspberries, blueberries)
- 200ml double cream
- 1 tbsp icing sugar

NUTRITION FACTS PER 100G:
Energy: 200 kcal | Protein: 2.5g | Total Fat: 10g | Saturated Fat: 6g |
Carbohydrates: 24g | Sugars: 23g | Dietary Fibre: 1g |

PREPARATION:

1. Begin by preheating your air fryer to 100°C.
2. In a large, clean mixing bowl, whisk the egg whites until soft peaks form.
3. Gradually add the caster sugar, one tablespoon at a time, whisking continuously until stiff peaks form.
4. Once the meringue is glossy, gently fold in the vanilla extract and white vinegar.
5. Spoon the meringue mixture into nests on a baking paper, ensuring an indentation in the centre of each nest.
6. Carefully place the meringue nests into the preheated air fryer and cook for 60 minutes until crisp.
7. While the meringues cool, whip the double cream with the icing sugar until soft peaks form.
8. Prepare the mixed berries by washing and slicing them as needed.
9. When the meringue nests have cooled, fill each one with a dollop of whipped cream and top with the prepared mixed berries.
10. Serve immediately and enjoy your delightful airy meringue nests with berries!

FLUFFY BANANA BREAD SQUARES

Servings: 9 | Difficulty: Easy | Temperature: 170°C |
Preparation Time: 10 minutes | Cooking Time: 25 minutes

INGREDIENTS:

- 3 ripe bananas (mashed)
- 100g granulated sugar
- 75g unsalted butter (melted)
- 1 tsp vanilla extract
- 1 large egg
- 125g plain flour
- 1 tsp baking powder
- 1/2 tsp baking soda
- 1/4 tsp salt
- 50ml milk

NUTRITION FACTS PER 100G:
Energy: 245 kcal | Protein: 3g | Total Fat: 7g | Saturated Fat: 4g |
Carbohydrates: 42g | Sugars: 22g | Dietary Fibre: 1.5g |

PREPARATION:

1. Begin by preheating your air fryer to 170°C.
2. In a large mixing bowl, combine the mashed bananas, granulated sugar, melted butter, vanilla extract, and egg. Mix well until fully amalgamated.
3. In a separate bowl, whisk together the plain flour, baking powder, baking soda, and salt.
4. Gradually add the dry ingredients to the wet mixture, folding in until just combined.
5. Pour in the milk and gently mix until the batter is smooth.
6. Line the air fryer basket with parchment paper.
7. Transfer the banana bread batter into the air fryer basket, spreading it evenly.
8. Air fry for about 25 minutes or until a skewer inserted in the centre comes out clean.
9. Once done, allow the banana bread to cool slightly before cutting into squares.
10. Serve warm and enjoy!

CINNAMON RAISIN BREAD PUDDING

Servings: 4 | Difficulty: Easy | Temperature: 160°C |
Preparation Time: 10 minutes | Cooking Time: 20 minutes

INGREDIENTS:

- 200g stale bread, cubed
- 100g raisins
- 2 large eggs
- 300ml whole milk
- 50g granulated sugar
- 1 tsp ground cinnamon
- 1 tsp vanilla extract
- 25g unsalted butter, melted
- 2 tbsp icing sugar, for dusting

NUTRITION FACTS PER 100G:
Energy: 210 kcal | Protein: 5g | Total Fat: 6g | Saturated Fat: 3.5g |
Carbohydrates: 34g | Sugars: 18g | Dietary Fibre: 2g

PREPARATION:

1. Preheat the air fryer to 160°C.
2. In a large mixing bowl, combine the cubed bread and raisins.
3. In a separate bowl, whisk together the eggs, whole milk, granulated sugar, ground cinnamon, and vanilla extract until well mixed.
4. Pour the egg mixture over the bread and raisins, and stir gently to combine.
5. Allow the mixture to sit for 5 minutes, letting the bread absorb the liquid.
6. Grease an air fryer-safe baking dish with the melted butter.
7. Transfer the soaked bread mixture into the prepared baking dish, spreading it evenly.
8. Place the dish into the air fryer and cook for 20 minutes, or until the top is golden and the middle is set.
9. Once cooked, remove from the air fryer and let stand for 5 minutes before serving.
10. Dust with icing sugar before serving, if desired.

ETON MESS WITH AIR-FRIED MERINGUES

Servings: 4 | Difficulty: Medium | Temperature: 120°C |
Preparation Time: 20 minutes | Cooking Time: 60 minutes

INGREDIENTS:

- 3 large egg whites
- 160g caster sugar
- 300ml double cream
- 1 tsp vanilla extract
- 300g strawberries, hulled and chopped
- 2 tbsp icing sugar

NUTRITION FACTS PER 100G:
Energy: 180 kcal | Protein: 2.5g | Total Fat: 12g | Saturated Fat: 7.5g |
Carbohydrates: 15g | Sugars: 14g | Dietary Fibre: 1g |

PREPARATION:

1. Preheat your air fryer to 120°C.
2. In a clean bowl, whisk egg whites until they form stiff peaks.
3. Gradually add caster sugar, continuing to whisk until the mixture is glossy.
4. Line the air fryer basket with parchment paper.
5. Spoon or pipe small dollops of the meringue mixture onto the parchment paper.
6. Cook in the air fryer for 60 minutes or until meringues are crisp on the outside.
7. While the meringues are cooking, whip the double cream with vanilla extract until soft peaks form.
8. Mix the chopped strawberries with icing sugar and set aside.
9. Once the meringues are ready, let them cool completely.
10. To assemble, layer crushed meringues, whipped cream, and strawberries in serving glasses.
11. Garnish with extra crushed meringues and strawberry pieces before serving.

CHOCOLATE-DIPPED FLAPJACKS

Servings: 12 Flapjacks | Difficulty: Easy | Temperature: 180°C |
Preparation Time: 15 minutes | Cooking Time: 20 minutes

INGREDIENTS:

- 200g rolled oats
- 125g unsalted butter
- 125g brown sugar
- 100g golden syrup
- 100g dark chocolate
- 2 tbsp whole milk

NUTRITION FACTS PER 100G:
Energy: 440 kcal | Protein: 4g | Total Fat: 22g | Saturated Fat: 12g |
Carbohydrates: 60g | Sugars: 35g | Dietary Fibre: 4g |

PREPARATION:

1. Start by lining the base of the air fryer basket with baking parchment.
2. Proceed by melting the butter, brown sugar, and golden syrup together in a saucepan over low heat, stirring until smooth.
3. Remove the saucepan from heat then mix in the rolled oats until well coated.
4. Fill the lined air fryer basket with the oat mixture, pressing firmly to create an even layer.
5. Set the air fryer to 180°C and cook for approximately 15-20 minutes, or until golden and firm.
6. Allow the cooked flapjack to cool completely on a wire rack.
7. While the flapjacks cool, melt the dark chocolate in a microwave-safe bowl, heating in 30-second intervals and stirring in between until fully melted.
8. Stir the whole milk into the melted chocolate until it achieves a smooth consistency.
9. Once the flapjacks have cooled, slice them into squares or rectangles, then dip each piece partially in the melted chocolate.
10. Place the chocolate-dipped flapjacks on a baking parchment to set.

DISCLAIMER

The information and recipes provided in *The XXL Air Fryer Recipe Book UK* are for general informational and culinary purposes only. While we have made every effort to ensure the accuracy of nutritional facts and ingredient lists, individual results may vary based on the specific air fryer model, ingredient brands, and personal dietary needs.

This book is not intended to provide medical or nutritional advice, and readers should consult with a healthcare professional or a registered dietitian before making significant changes to their diet, particularly if they have food allergies, medical conditions, or specific nutritional requirements.

The author and publisher are not responsible for any adverse effects, allergic reactions, or health complications that may arise from using the recipes in this book. Readers are advised to carefully check all ingredients and exercise caution when trying new foods, especially when preparing meals for others.

All recipe results, including cooking times and textures, may differ based on variations in air fryer models and capacities. Always follow the manufacturer's guidelines for safe use of your air fryer.

This book is for personal use only, and any unauthorized reproduction, distribution, or commercial use of its contents is prohibited.

By using this book, readers agree to these terms and assume full responsibility for any culinary outcomes or dietary effects.

EXCLUSIVE BONUS

40 Weight Loss Recipes

&

14 Days Meal Plan

Scan the QR-Code and receive
the FREE download: